UNLOCKING THE POWER OF ARTIFICIAL INTELLIGENCE

AI SIMPLIFIED: A BEGINNER'S GUIDE TO UNLOCKING THE POWER OF ARTIFICIAL INTELLIGENCE FOR PRACTICAL KNOWLEDGE AND FUTURE-READY SKILLS

DECLAN MCKINLEY

© Copyright 2023 - All rights reserved.

The content contained within this book may not be reproduced, duplicated or transmitted without direct written permission from the author or the publisher.

Under no circumstances will any blame or legal responsibility be held against the publisher, or author, for any damages, reparation, or monetary loss due to the information contained within this book, either directly or indirectly.

Legal Notice:

This book is copyright protected. It is only for personal use. You cannot amend, distribute, sell, use, quote or paraphrase any part, or the content within this book, without the consent of the author or publisher.

Disclaimer Notice:

Please note the information contained within this document is for educational and entertainment purposes only. All effort has been executed to present accurate, up to date, reliable, complete information. No warranties of any kind are declared or implied. Readers acknowledge that the author is not engaged in the rendering of legal, financial, medical or professional advice. The content within this book has been derived from various sources. Please consult a licensed professional before attempting any techniques outlined in this book.

By reading this document, the reader agrees that under no circumstances is the author responsible for any losses, direct or indirect, that are incurred as a result of the use of the information contained within this document, including, but not limited to, errors, omissions, or inaccuracies.

CONTENTS

Introduction   5

1. AI FUNDAMENTALS   9
   History and Evolution of AI   10
   Types of AI Systems   18
   Understanding the Significance of AI in
   Automation and Decision-Making   24
   Key AI Terminology   26

2. UNRAVELING AI ALGORITHMS   31
   Exploring Supervised Learning   31
   Embracing Unsupervised Learning   34
   Navigating Reinforcement Learning   38

3. DATA AND AI—A SYMBIOTIC
   RELATIONSHIP   43
   The Role of Data in AI   43
   Big Data and AI   49
   Ethical Data Usage in AI   54

4. THE POWER OF NEURAL NETWORKS   61
   Anatomy of a Neural Network   61
   Training Neural Networks   65
   Types of Neural Networks   68

5. AI IN EVERYDAY LIFE   73
   Understanding NLP   74
   AI in Smart Homes and the Internet of
   Things   77
   AI in Healthcare and Medicine   82

6. THE FUTURE OF AI   87
   AI in Finance and Banking   87
   AI in Transportation and Logistics   91
   AI and Creativity   95

7. AI ETHICS AND RESPONSIBLE AI 101
   Bias and Fairness in AI 101
   AI Regulation and Governance 103
   The Future of Responsible AI 108

8. AI AND SOCIETY—OPPORTUNITIES AND
   CHALLENGES 113
   The Impact of AI on Jobs 113
   AI and Social Implications 117
   AI and Global Collaboration 121

9. AI AND THE HUMAN-MACHINE
   INTERFACE 127
   Explainable AI 127
   AI and Human Creativity 129
   AI and Emotional Intelligence 131

Conclusion 135
Bibliography 139

INTRODUCTION

At this point, I don't think anyone doubts the power of artificial intelligence (AI) and how it has already changed our everyday lives. The technology is already making a massive impact, and it still promises to completely revolutionize many aspects of our society, such as the way we work, the way we move, and the way we live.

We can look at almost any sector of our society, and we already see the direct impact of AI. For example, an action as simple as shopping online might have AI involved when the website suggests what you might like because it remembers your preferences and offers you suggestions on what you might like. When you check your email, the underlying software knows exactly what should go directly to the spam folder and what shouldn't.

Or when you're driving using a GPS on a congested road, it will tell you what other alternatives are there for you to get to your destination faster. Another great example of

INTRODUCTION

AI in our daily lives is your smartphone. You can simply call Siri, Alexa, or Bing Chat, depending on what smartphone brand you have, and ask anything.

Here, AI is working behind the scenes to give you answers based on previous conversations you've had with it. Or, more recently, Google's and Tesla's self-driving cars, which are totally controlled by AI. But AI is not only used for transportation or personal use. It's present in the advertising, financial, and even security sectors, among many others. AI is here to stay, and it has spread through most of our societal sectors.

However, some of the most important fields where AI is already present, but its impact will likely become more relevant and even change our future are, for example, in the healthcare field. We all know that healthcare costs are escalating and becoming a real issue for most families. AI can help by taking some of the burden off of doctors, but one of the most promising AI advantages in this sector is better diagnosis of diseases.

Machine learning, which is a subcategory of AI where the software is able to expand its knowledge based on experience and trial and error, will eventually become good enough to find diseases that we were not capable of and much faster than our human brains could. AI in the most diverse technology fields can also have a massive impact, whether it is on the climate change issue, cleaner energy, or mitigating the effects of poverty. AI is everywhere, and we will see significant beneficial changes in the coming years.

However, I understand that AI is still a subject where some people might be reluctant, or it might be a little confusing with all the different news and advancements coming out. This is why I wrote this book: to try and make sense of it all and to make AI more approachable and usable for readers regardless of their background. It's aimed at providing beginners with a simplified and accessible guide to understanding AI and empowering them with practical knowledge and future-ready skills to leverage the power of AI effectively.

We will start with the fundamentals of AI, looking at the different types of AI systems and basic terminology. Then, we will dive into what an AI algorithm is and what the purpose of machine learning and reinforcement learning is. We will move on to the symbiotic relationship between data and AI, the power of neural networks, how AI affects our everyday lives, what the future holds for us and AI, what AI ethics and responsible AI are, what the main challenges and opportunities are when AI is fully integrated into our society, and what is a human-machine interface.

Don't worry if you don't understand some of these terms; I will explain them in detail, and by the end of it, you will know everything that there is to know about how to leverage AI for your own benefit.

1

AI FUNDAMENTALS

AI is developing fast to the point that in a matter of years, we've had AI spread out into most sectors of our society, and it is now harder to find a field where AI has yet to make an impact. But it has gotten to a point where it is not only growing, it's exponentially growing. This can be linked to something called Moore's law, whereas technology grows, it doubles its advancements every few years. For example, let's assume a situation where there's some important information and only one person with this information.

For the sake of simplicity, this information travels slowly, and within a week, one person can only spread this information to two other people. In the 1st week, person 0 (the one with the original information) relays this information to 2 other people (person 1 and person 2). In the 2nd week, persons 1 and 2 relay this information to persons 3, 4, 5, and 6. This tells us that in the first week, this information was only given to two people, but in the second week, it was given to four people.

From here, it's easy to assume that in the 3rd week, this information will be given to 8 people, in the 4th week to 16 people, and so on. This is exponential growth, and this is how fast AI is moving into new sectors, new devices, new technologies, and so on. Of course, there are many more factors involved, which increase even more how quickly this growth happens, but we will be talking about this throughout the book. First, let's look at the history and origin of AI.

HISTORY AND EVOLUTION OF AI

At the start of the 20th century, the general public started to get familiarized with science fiction and, at the same time, with the concept of AI. Curiously, one of the first mainstream interactions with both of these concepts, even though at the time they were not as defined, was with the heartless Tin Man from *The Wizard of Oz*. Twenty-five years later, *Metropolis* came out with a humanoid robot. But it wasn't until around the 1950s that mathematicians, philosophers, and scientists had their take on the subject and created the concept of AI, which began to be assimilated by the masses.

One of the most important advocates of the concept of AI was a young British mathematician called Alan Turing, who combined mathematics with AI. Essentially, he asked: "If humans use available information to come up with solutions to problems, why can't computers do the same?"

This was better explained in his paper, "Computing Machinery and Intelligence," where he talked about how people could build intelligent machinery and test their intelligence. However, at the time, there were many things objecting to his thinking and his decision to actually pursue what he had written.

One of those things was a better computer, or computers that at least had the precondition for intelligence. At the time, computers couldn't even save commands, and their only function was to execute them, which essentially meant that computers could do things but couldn't remember things to do later, so every command had to be done right away. Also, at the time, computers were very expensive, even to rent, and only certain large tech companies and universities had them.

But not everything was bad news, and a few years later, Allen Newell, Herbert Simon, and Cliff Shaw began the proof of concept with a program called Logic Theorist, which was programmed to imitate the problem-solving abilities of a person. This is considered to be the very first AI program to ever exist, and it was presented in 1956. While the conference somehow fell short of the organizers' expectations, mainly because people could come and go as they intended, it's now seen as a historical conference that started the ball rolling when it came to the advancement of AI in the next two decades.

From the 1950s until the 1970s, AI continued to be talked about and evolved. At this point, computers were more powerful, faster, cheaper, and could store more information. With this, another subtopic of AI—machine learning—started to flourish, especially when it came to these machines learning different algorithms and what algorithm to use for the different problems presented.

A few experiments showed promise when it came to interpreting spoken language and other general problem-solving issues, which allowed government-backed as well as private companies to fund AI research. While everything seemed to go according to plan, there was still a very long way for AI to develop to the point that it could reach abstract thinking, self-recognition, or natural language processing (NLP). In fact, during that time, the more scientists and researchers learned about it, the more obstacles presented themselves. One of these obstacles, perhaps the largest of them all, was computational power.

While computers could now store information, they couldn't store enough or process it fast enough to reach the goals researchers had in mind. Because computers were nowhere near that power, patience started to thin with those who funded AI projects, and in turn, so did the funding. This made AI technology slow down for a whole decade.

However, by the 1980s, curiosity had been rekindled once more through increased algorithms and an increase in funds. This was mostly done thanks to a method made known by David Rumelhart and John Hopfield called "deep learning" (DL), which simply allows computers to learn through their past experiences, just like a person does.

In a different experiment, Edward Feigenbaum created something called an expert system, which allowed computers to mirror the process of decision-making by expert humans. This essentially allowed computers to learn from an expert in a field. At the time, some governments, in particular the Japanese government, invested in these expert systems and other AI experiments with the aim of radically transforming computer processing; however, the main goals were never achieved, and once again, AI's hype fell.

But, despite the lack of funding, AI continued to evolve. Between the 1990s and the 2000s, things were going well for AI as researchers reached impressive milestones. For instance, the infamous defeat of world chess champion Garry Kasparov by IBM's Deep Blue brought media and public attention to AI again. In 1998, speech recognition software designed by Dragon System was introduced to Windows computers.

As you know, Moore's Law states that the speed and capacity of computers doubles every year, which means that we no longer have an issue with computer storage. We just had to wait until the capacity surpassed the needs we had, which it did. Many say that we are living in what is called the "big data" age, where we have the ability to gather large amounts of data that we, the people, can no longer process, so we are turning to AI, and it's been quite successful in that regard across many different sectors and industries. Because of machine learning, even if the algorithms we use don't change as much, AI continues to learn.

So, what do we expect to see in the future? In the near future, AI language seems to be what's catching everyone's eye, and there are many different and successful applications in that regard, whether it is ChatGPT or anything similar to it, or chatbots to get through a company's customer service. On another note, driverless cars also seem to be on the rise, and we can already see some of that happening.

In the long term, we can expect AI to become more advanced than us in many regards; perhaps sentient AI will become too much like those sci-fi movies we like so much, or at least an iteration of it. However, even if we have the technology to create them in the next decade, there are too many ethical questions that we need to answer first, so this type of advancement might take a little longer. However, in the next few years, we will see tremendous improvement in the AI sector and every single sector AI is incorporated into.

The Emergence of DL and Neural Networks

DL is part of the machine learning area, but it's somehow a little more advanced in terms of how knowledge is absorbed by any type of machine. It uses several layers of algorithms to process data and mimic our own thinking processes. In very simple terms, the way it works is that data passes through each layer, and the outcome of the previous layer is the input for the next one. Since the first layer is called the input layer (because that's where information is added, and the last is the output layer), every other layer in between is called the hidden layer, and each layer has an algorithm that performs a single function.

There's another main feature of DL that is often used for pattern recognition as well as image processing called feature extraction, which is usually done for learning or training purposes. The first advancements in the field of DL started in 1943 when Warren McCulloch and Walter Pitts came up with a computer that was heavily based on the human brain, specifically its neural network. Again, they tried to mimic human thought processes using an algorithm, and from there, DL became an established field.

In the 1960s, there were quite some advances in the field, especially with a model called the Back Propagation Model, developed by Henry J. Kelley. Two years later, Stuart Dreyfus came up with a much simpler version of that model, but essentially, this model allowed for the backward propagation of errors, so machines could be better trained; however, we had to wait until the 1980s to have a much more efficient version of it.

During the 1970s, there was somehow a lack of results, and many promises made years prior didn't happen, mainly because of a lack of funding from both AI and DL. Amid this uncertainty, some researchers continued their work. Kunihiko Fukushima, a Japanese computer scientist, was the first to design convolutional neural networks where there were several pooling and convolutional layers, and a few years later, in 1979, he designed Neocognitron, which was an artificial neural network using multilayered and hierarchical design. This allowed computers to recognize and learn certain visual patterns.

During the following years, many of the Neocognitron ideas continued to be used in pursuing more evolved AI systems. But other concepts, such as new learning methods, allowed the creation of many different neural networks that evolved from the Neocognitron.

One such model used the selective attention concept, which allowed the AI to shift attention from one task to the next, much like we do when we multitask. Other models could "infer," which means that if information was missing, they could not only identify it but also complete it with new information. During these years, there was also a learning technique that continued to progress called backpropagation, where the use of errors could be used to train DL models, but this wasn't used in neural networks until the mid-1980s when three scientists placed backpropagation in a neural network with interesting results.

During the 1980s and 1990s, there were some advancements in the field, such as Yann LeCun's first practical demonstration of backpropagation, where he blended back propagation and a convolutional neural network to read handwritten numbers. However, between 1985 and 1990, the second AI winter happened, where a lack of funding was notorious and affected research in the field. This was mainly due to many researchers and other individuals who exaggerated the potential of AI at the time and believed AI would have an impact right away, which broke investors' expectations.

In fact, this feeling was so strong that, at some point, both AI and DL were considered pseudoscience. However, some other researchers continue to work on these fields and quickly reach some considerable advancements. For instance, in 1995, Vladimir Vapnik and Dana Cortes created the vector machine, which was initially used to map and identify similar data.

Two years later, Sepp Hochreiter and Juergen Schmidhuber developed long-short-term memory (LSTM). This was an important step, especially for DL, and in 1999, computers started to become more powerful, with more potential to advance in the AI and DL fields. It was around this time that both vector machines and neural networks started to compete with one another, and while the vector machine was faster, the neural network offered better results overall while using the same data.

However, in the early 2000s, another problem appeared, which is often called the Vanishing Gradient Problem, and this essentially stated that upper layers did not learn features (or lessons) because these weren't being passed from the lower layers. This meant that there was no learning signal coming from the lower layers and that it could not reach the upper layers. While this wasn't a problem that affected all the neural networks and only the ones using gradient-based learning methods, it still remained a problem, and it was later found that there was a problem with the activation functions. Then, two solutions were presented: by doing layer-by-layer pre-training or using LSTM.

In the early 2010s, the graphics processing unit (commonly known as the GPU) speed had increased so much that it was possible to train neural networks without the need for layer-by-layer training, and because of that, DL started to become more and more significant when it came to speed and efficiency. Google Brain was released in 2012 and with that, the outcomes of a project called "The Cat Experiment," which highlighted the problems with unsupervised learning, which essentially meant that until that point, the neural network could be taught only using labeled data but now could be fed unlabeled data.

The researchers used unlabeled images taken from YouTube videos to train the software, and in the end, one of the highest layers of the neural network responded strongly to images of cats (hence, the name of the experiment), but it also responded well to images of people's faces, which marked a great advance in the DL space. In 2014, the Generative Adversarial Neural Network was introduced, and in this experiment, two neural networks played against one another in a game with the objective that one of the networks mimicked a photo and tricked the other into believing the other was real.

TYPES OF AI SYSTEMS

There are two main types of AI that we will be looking at: narrow AI and general AI. While narrow AI is developed to solve a single problem or perform a single action, such as a chatbot, general or artificial general intelligence (AGI) is a more generalized AI and can solve many different problems. It's important to note that AGI is still only theoretical, but it's getting closer to materializing.

Narrow AI

Narrow AI, also known as artificial narrow intelligence, or even weak AI, is any AI that can exceed human performance in a single task. It's only designed for that specific task, and it has many limitations. This type of AI is stimulated by human behavior, cannot think for itself, and has well-defined rules and contexts when training. For instance, machine learning is a form of narrow AI. Let's see more examples.

One of the most common examples of narrow AI is searching the internet. For instance, the Google RankBrain algorithm uses narrow AI to understand queries and the intent of the user for better search results. Another use of narrow AI is for disease detection. This is because this type of AI can process a large amount of information in a short time, which makes it faster and often more accurate than healthcare professionals when it comes to disease diagnosis.

The recommender system is also one of the most common narrow AI uses, especially in services such as Netflix or Spotify, and it is used to find recommended shows or songs, in this particular case just by using information related to the user's behavior. Facial recognition is becoming more prevalent and is often used to provide authentication. And despite the fact that when it comes to identification, they outperform humans, they are still lagging behind in other aspects such as processing vague images, which still limits their use in other areas such as investigation work.

Narrow AI brings many benefits to society, and every success in this field is another step forward toward AGI. As we've seen, narrow AI makes certain tasks far more efficient and workers more productive. While in the media AI is being linked to large-scale redundancies, the truth is that it is helping a lot of others do their jobs better as well as alleviating their work. When it comes to decision-making, because of AI's analytical skills, workers become better at making decisions, especially if we add the fact that AI is devoid of emotions and can make more logical decisions.

Narrow AI also offers a much better customer experience and once again alleviates workers, especially if we look at chatbots, which can filter customers in the first phase to narrow down the issues they have and point workers to help them faster. Recommender systems also improve customer experiences and allow them to find better solutions.

General AI

General AI is often called strong AI because it allows machines to be proficient in a varied number of skills. If we look at narrow AI, it can only function in a particular environment and do the same tasks over and over again. With general AI, the goal is to create something that can actually reason just like a person would. This is where the AI fields want to go and what they are trying to achieve in the long run. It's not possible at the moment to simply replicate the human brain because it's far too complex.

However, advancements are coming fast and we are narrowing the gap. Some examples of general AI are, for example, more advanced chatbots, especially those that use NLP, to understand what we are saying and respond accordingly. This type of general AI, in this context, would be able to come up with a response without relying on other information or other responses.

Autonomous vehicles are yet another example of general AI, and we have some large companies working on this, such as Uber or Tesla, and some have achieved quite an impressive level. Tesla in particular has achieved what is called Level 4 automation, which is when a car can operate by itself but only under certain circumstances. The last level is 5, and that would be a vehicle that could act with intuit in any context without any intervention by a human, but this is really hard to reach because it requires the AI to deal with all types of environments that could possibly happen during its journey.

When comparing narrow and general AI, there are many things that separate the two. One of the most impressive ones is that general AI would not require programming from humans, as well as being able to respond to any scenario or situation and adapt quickly to anything. This means that a general AI would almost have the brain of a person, with background knowledge and even common sense. While narrow AI needs programming, the data has to be labeled, and it uses predefined rules to achieve its tasks.

Exploring AI Applications in Robotics, NLP, and Computer Vision

Even though AI is a relatively new space, it already has many different applications in the most diverse realms. This becomes even more apparent when we divide the three AI fields and try to understand their applications. In this section, we will be looking at AI applications in robotics, NLP, and computer vision.

I've already mentioned a few applications AI can have in the field of robotics, such as autonomous vehicles, especially in using it coupled with sensors, such as radar, cameras, or lidar, and AI algorithms to allow the processing of sensor data to understand the surrounding environment, which in turn allows for real-time decisions allowing for safe navigation without the intervention of a person. But there are many more. For instance, in the medical field, it can be used to power surgical robots, particularly during delicate procedures. These algorithms improve the surgeon's precision and stabilize hand tremors.

Industrial automation is also another field where AI can shine in relation to robotics. For instance, AI-powered robots in manufacturing can perform tasks that require high precision, such as welding, quality control, or assembling products. In the social robot field, these robots powered by AI can understand emotions, create human speech, and engage in conversations. Or even in the drone field, where AI-powered drones can do a myriad of things such as search and rescue operations, surveillance, and even delivery services. In the same way, AI can be used in agricultural robotics to remove weeds, apply the right amount of fertilizer, or harvest crops.

When it comes to AI applications in NLP, perhaps this is where the field is more advanced. Most AI virtual assistants and chatbots are NLP-driven. These types of chatbots allow personalization for the client, such as in answering inquiries or providing customer support that allows users to go through many different processes, which also improves the user experience and decreases human intervention. In translation, AI is taking over the field, and there are many systems that allow accurate translation, such as Transformers (a machine-learning model).

The same is happening with text generation with the likes of GPT-3 or 4, which, more recently, can create consistent and relevant text. There's another field when it comes to AI applications in NLP, which is sentiment analysis, where AI can analyze text to understand sentiments such as negative, neutral, or positive, which might be of great use to understand all types of feedback, social trends, or public opinion. Lastly, another field where NLP-driven AI is doing great is speech recognition, where algorithms have the power to convert spoken language into written text that can be used in voice commands or voice assistants.

In computer vision, AI is also an increasing trend. One of the most popular is facial recognition, where AI, through algorithms, can recognize and analyze facial features, which can be used for authentication or security access. In image classification, AI can classify images and objects. One of the most important aspects of AI in computer vision is in medical imaging, where it can help diagnose and analyze MRIs, CT scans, or X-rays, for instance. But perhaps the most advanced AI application in this field is in virtual reality and augmented reality, which allows for tracking real-world objects or creating immersive virtual reality or augmented reality immersive environments.

UNDERSTANDING THE SIGNIFICANCE OF AI IN AUTOMATION AND DECISION-MAKING

The significance of AI in both automation and decision-making is tremendous, to the point that it is revolutionizing whole industries, impacting efficiency, and allowing people to make more informed decisions.

Let's start with automation. As we've seen, AI can be extremely important when it comes to productivity and efficiency. For instance, AI-driven automation can decrease human intervention in repetitive tasks, which leads to an increase in efficiency since it frees up time for workers and because AI can perform these tasks much faster. The consistency of these AIs as well as the quality they present minimize mistakes that before were attributed to worker fatigue, which is extremely important in sectors such as manufacturing.

AI also allows companies to scale their businesses without the need to hire new workers, mainly because it allows these companies to automate systems and cope with higher volumes of assignments without increasing the cost. And this brings us to another significant aspect, which is cost savings. While there's a significant initial investment in this technology, in the long run, it saves money. Another important aspect here is that AI-powered systems allow for 24/7 operations, which is absolutely vital for some companies in certain industries where continuous processes are vital.

AI is also very significant in decision-making. For example, in risk assessment, AI can evaluate risks and come up with predictions for potential outcomes by going through historical data, which is relevant to the insurance and financial market industries. This is also great for data analysis, where AI can go through large amounts of data to understand trends and patterns that workers might miss, making decision-making far more accurate.

It's also important for marketing personalization, where AI is able to analyze behaviors and come up with better recommendations, which leads to higher customer engagement and satisfaction. In this particular case, AI can also give real-time insights because it can process real-time data, which is especially crucial for sectors such as stock trading. When it comes to decision-making, one of the best uses of AI, which is extremely significant, is in resolving complex problems. Because it can analyze large amounts of data, it can aid in situations where there are many different variables.

KEY AI TERMINOLOGY

Before we delve into more about how AI works and the power it has, I believe that we need to define some terminology to make sure the following chapters are well understood. Let's first go through the foundations, such as terms like machine learning, algorithms, and data sets.

As I've explained before, machine learning (from now on, I'll abbreviate it to ML) is a subset of AI that encompasses the evolution of models and algorithms that allow computers to understand and make decisions or predictions based on data fed into these algorithms without the need for particular programming for the different processes it has to go through. Essentially, ML means that computers can learn as more knowledge is fed into them and improve over time.

The main goal of ML is to create algorithms that can learn better and faster with the data given to them. The only way to do this is through the training of these algorithms within a dataset that has examples and outcomes from these examples. The more data it processes, the more the algorithm is able to make better decisions and predictions later. ML can be defined into three major categories, and I've already mentioned some of them: supervised learning, unsupervised learning, and reinforcement learning.

Supervised learning happens when the algorithm trains with the help of labeled datasets where all the examples have corresponding outcomes. So, here, the algorithm is learning the inputs and the outputs and making predictions based on those examples. Unsupervised learning means that the dataset fed into the algorithm is not labeled, and it needs to find the outcomes, such as structures and patterns, with the dataset given. Lastly, reinforcement learning means that the algorithm learns through trial and error and adjusts its predictions and decisions based on the outcomes.

In essence, AI algorithms are processes and instructions in a computer, allowing AI machines to do certain tasks, make predictions, or make decisions that have the ability to replace humans or human intelligence. These algorithms are created to understand patterns, create insights, and process data, which allows machines to imitate human thinking and behavior. As we've seen above, algorithms can be supervised, unsupervised, or reinforcement learning algorithms, but they can also be NLP, computer vision, DL, evolutionary, or recommendation algorithms, among others.

Datasets are compiled and organized data points, arranged in a way that allows easy pattern recognition and analysis. Each data point is a different observation, and each of them provides crucial information. These data points can be literally anything, such as descriptions, classifications, measurements, and so forth. Essentially, it's an assembly of information. To give you an example, with supervised algorithms (where data is labeled), these datasets show correct outcomes. Datasets are vital to performing scientific research and other analyses that allow the training of these machines, and they are categorized differently depending on their intended use.

Datasets can also come from anywhere, such as sensors, surveys, or many other sources.

AI and Ethical Training

The ethical training of AI is extremely important for many different reasons that I will discuss in this section, but one of the most relevant ones is, so it can make unbiased decisions and analyses. However, it goes way beyond that. Training data is vital for AI systems, and not only any data but also the diversity, quantity, and quality of that data can influence the accuracy of the AI analysis. Let's see other reasons why data, and in this particular case, training data, is so relevant.

AI models that are trained with good-quality training data are more likely to extrapolate unseen data, which helps with any type of variation that the AI might find when analyzing real-life situations. Everything the AI model learns comes from its learned relationships and patterns in training data, and the more extensive that data is, the better the AI will perform. Having diverse data is also crucial because it allows the AI to be ready for more complex problem-solving as well as adapt better when its datasets are updated.

When it comes to ethical considerations, it's crucial that this data be diverse because it can have a tremendous impact on certain individuals and even industries. So, when considering ethical factors, things like privacy, transparency, fairness, and accountability are relevant. For example, when it comes to privacy, training data might have some sensitive personal information; hence, this data should receive protection, so it doesn't fall within privacy violations. The same is true for transparency, and here, users should know how AI makes their decisions. For that, there needs to be transparent models that allow great insight into how AI makes its predictions.

This comes from data collection, which is just as relevant. When collecting data to be fed into AI algorithms, it's important that this aligns with ethical standards. If not, this can lead to malicious purposes, such as cyberattacks or the dissemination of misinformation. An example of how AI ethical considerations are important is through an AI recruiter screening tool that sorts recruiters in the first phase, and if this AI is not up to ethical standards, it can lead to the job displacement of certain individuals. Tackling these issues requires industry experts, researchers, and policymakers to be able to design guidelines and regulations that ensure AI is created ethically and responsibly.

We've seen how dynamic the AI field can be and how it is influencing our society. The rapid growth of AI is similar to how Moore's law is described, and it is quickly reaching many different industries and sectors. From the very beginning, around the 20th century, AI has developed through many key milestones, including the influence of Alan Turing and the rise of DL and neural networks that allowed us to have the AI we have today. We've also analyzed the two different categories of AI, narrow AI, and general AI, that explain different features of the AI realm.

With narrow AI, we can accomplish specific tasks, while with general AI, we get closer to human intelligence. We've also seen the many different applications of AI, such as in robotics, NLP, or computer vision. But one of the most important achievements of AI is its power for automation and how it can streamline operations to alleviate the burden on workers, as well as how it can simplify decision-making through analysis, which in turn has a massive impact in many different industries.

AI's rapid growth and multifaceted applications are here to stay and have already reshaped many sectors and industries. As we continue to advance in this field, we have to give more relevance to other aspects, such as ethical considerations, and make sure AI is developed responsibly, so we can continue to enjoy AI's potential. As we progress through the book, I will simplify complex AI concepts to show you that they are not as difficult to understand as you might have thought. In the following chapter, we will delve into AI algorithms and explore their many different types of learning.

2

UNRAVELING AI ALGORITHMS

According to Statista, by 2025, the global AI software market is forecast to grow to $126 billion, and it is predicted that it will continue to grow after that (Thormundsson, 2022). In this chapter, we will unravel AI algorithms and go a little beyond what we've already mentioned by exploring ML a little better and diving deeper into supervised, unsupervised, and reinforcement learning to understand how plausible this statistic might be.

EXPLORING SUPERVISED LEARNING

I've already mentioned the three types of learning algorithms used: supervised learning, unsupervised learning, and reinforcement learning, but we will now try to understand the concept of labeled data and unlabeled data, what their roles are in AI training, and showcase some real-world examples.

When exploring supervised learning in AI and ML, the most crucial aspect is labeled data because it's the fundamental aspect of this type of learning. Labeled data is vital for training models to make decisions, predictions, and classifications that are accurate. As you know, labeled data is a type of dataset where each different data point is linked to a known category, or label (hence the name), which allows AI models to follow it as a guide.

When going through the processes of training AI with labeled data, this allows it to understand relationships and patterns and, as a result, be able to define different categories, which in turn allows for the learning process to be generalized and allows it to understand new data and make accurate predictions on it. So, in other words, labeled data gives a framework for AI learning models and how these models can understand decisions and how to make them.

For example, if there's a task with a dataset labeled "images of people," these images would have related labels such as the different characteristics of people (like race, hair color, height, etc.), this allows the model to understand the different characteristics of what they are analyzing (which in this case would be people) and attribute it or understand it. This is why diversity and quality of labeled data are so important for training because people have many different characteristics, and when AI is presented with any image of a person, they will be able to characterize it. But as you might have guessed, preparing these datasets can be a tedious process, especially if it's a high-quality dataset where all data points have to be properly labeled.

When you hear "regression" and "classification," these are types of algorithms that are used to create models on labeled data for training. As you might have guessed, they work in different ways because their purposes are a little different, but both have rooted their training principles in supervised learning. Regression algorithms are often used when the variable you are trying to get is a numeric value that is also continuous. These regression algorithms try to establish a relationship between the target variables and the independent variables.

With these two points, the AI tries to make predictions based on new data points. Let me explain how these types of algorithms work to try and make better sense of it. During the training phase, regression algorithms analyze the labeled training data and find the best solution that is able to describe the relationship between the two targets. During the prediction phase (meaning that the algorithm is already trained), the algorithm can find results on new data points. Examples of regression-type algorithms support vector regressions or linear regressions and are used for things like predicting temperatures, the stock market, or even house prices.

Classification algorithms, as the name suggests, are often used when the target is a category, and their goal is to grab results and place them in different classes. During the training phase, the AI algorithm examines the labeled training data to understand relationships and patterns and try to find out about optimal decisions. During the prediction phase, this model is able to be used as a prediction AI through class labels on new data points. These types of algorithms can come in many different forms, such as decision trees or support vector machines, and they are often used to detect spam, classify images, or diagnose diseases, among other uses.

To sum up, regression algorithms can predict numeric values such as temperatures or stock market values, and classification algorithms are often used to categorize and classify.

As I've said, there are many uses for supervised learning in the real world, such as stock price prediction, image classification, or medical diagnosis, but there are others. For instance, email spam detection is one of them. This is a classification algorithm that detects spam emails from labeled datasets. Here, the algorithm separates the spam emails from the nonspam emails every time there's a new email. Banks use supervised learning in their algorithms to predict their clients' credit scores when it comes to giving loans. Speech recognition is also supervised learning, like Apple's Siri, which learns from spoken audio samples. As you can see, supervised learning is incredibly versatile, and it can be used in the most diverse industries and sectors where labeled training data can be used.

EMBRACING UNSUPERVISED LEARNING

Unsupervised learning is used in AI when it is tasked with identifying patterns in a dataset when not presented with labels. This is different from supervised learning because it learns from data that is already labeled. However, when there's no predefined labeled data, an unsupervised learning approach is preferable. There are two main applications when using unsupervised learning: anomaly detection and clustering. The first usually involves identifying unusual passages in a dataset that diverge from what is expected, and here, an AI algorithm that learns from unsupervised approaches can identify patterns that are not within the norms.

Some real-life examples of anomaly detection are financial fraud or faulty products because these deviate from the norm and are then anomalous. Clustering is when the algorithm groups data that is identical based on its characteristics. Here, the algorithm analyzes the data and can understand its natural clusters within unlabeled data, which means it naturally understands where each piece of data belongs. One example of this is when the algorithm tries to group different customers' purchase behavior and do it solely based on their habits, which then allows them to target those customers with certain ads.

As you might imagine, there are many different applications for unsupervised learning, especially in data analysis and recommendation systems. When it comes to recommendation systems, this often involves the recommendation of products, content, or even services based on behaviors or preferences. These are often used in marketing and advertising for streaming system recommendations like Netflix or Spotify. Within recommendation systems, there are a few techniques.

For instance, topic modeling is often used for content recommendation, where the algorithm is able to analyze text data to find fundamental topics that are then used to recommend content based on the user's preferences and interests. There's also another technique called principal component analysis that allows for more efficiency when making recommendations, or even collaborative filtering, where the algorithm determines users that have similar preferences based on their interactions, which allows for more personalized recommendations.

Data analysis in unsupervised learning is a great way to understand datasets that are quite complex. Within these techniques, there's anomaly detection and clustering analysis, as we've seen, but also market basket analysis, where the algorithm can analyze and identify transactional data and is often used in the retail sector to improve promotions and product placements.

Unsupervised learning has its advantages and disadvantages. When it comes to advantages, the one that stands out the most is the absence of the requirement of labeled data, which is often a process that is quite time-consuming and expensive. It provides a great tool when it comes to exploring data and finding patterns that are not easily perceived.

As I've mentioned, it allows for anomaly detection, cluster analysis, and feature extraction—which allows for the extraction of meaningful features in the underlying data, and data preprocessing, where unsupervised learning can aid in data preprocessing by finding out any values that might be missing. One other advantage of unsupervised learning is adaptability, where this approach is able to handle changing and diverse data without any need for retraining.

When it comes to disadvantages, unsupervised learning algorithms also have a few, such as difficulty in interpretation. This means that this algorithmic approach can come up with complex outputs, but these outputs can be hard to come by and interpret, especially when there's a nonlinear relationship within the data. Because unsupervised learning doesn't need labels, it might be hard to validate how accurate the results might be. This is especially true when we compare it to supervised learning, where it is easier to predict outcomes because they are known and labeled.

Another issue with unsupervised learning approaches is the fact that this unlabeled data might have noisy data, which might affect the capture of relevant data, and consequently the whole process.

Unsupervised data is a powerful tool, especially when the datasets from which the data points come are not labeled, and while there might be some challenges, especially in the interpretation and validation of these outcomes, it also has plenty of advantages, such as anomaly detection or exploratory analysis, which might be essential in certain circumstances.

NAVIGATING REINFORCEMENT LEARNING

Reinforcement learning (from now on, RL), is a subset of ML where an AI-driven system, also known as an agent, can learn through trial and error using feedback from the actions performed. One of the main concepts of reinforcement learning is the agent itself, which is when AI learns to cooperate with the environment itself, and its actions are based on observations. The environment is the external system with which the agent interacts. This means that the past actions of the agent allow for feedback.

There's also a reward, which is a value given by the environment to point out how desirable the actions of the agent are. The goal of the agent, in this case, is to perform actions that maximize rewards over time. So, essentially, the AI is learning through rewards or penalties for its actions.

RL is linked to AI agents because it allows for training agents to make optimized decisions in the long term. Just like people learn from trial and error, in this case, it is similar. The more actions the agent performs, the more it knows, and the more this experience guides the AI's decision-making. RL can be seen in many sectors and industries, such as autonomous vehicles, recommendation systems, and even robotics.

Let's look at some examples of RL in games and robotics control. For example, in gaming, Dota 2, a popular action real-time strategy video game, and OpenAI, the realtors of

ChatGPT, created an AI bot for the game called Open AI's Dota 2 Bot that understood how to play the game and also competed with other professional players through RL.

The Deep Q-Network is an algorithm created by Atari Games that learned how to play classic Atari games through simple observation. In robotics, we have the popular example of autonomous cars, where RL is able to train self-driving cars to make different decisions in many real-life scenarios. Drone flights are another example of robotics, where RL allows drones to learn complicated flight exercises.

Finally, let's focus on RL in autonomous systems since it seems to be one of the largest developments in the field and look at its potential. In autonomous vehicles, as we've seen, RL can be used to train self-driving cars and allow them to make the best possible decisions when performing the task of driving. The RL algorithm behind this allows vehicles to not only become efficient but also learn how to drive safely. We can go a little further into the potential of RL algorithms and look at how smart cities would behave as taught by RL.

Such algorithms could optimize the city infrastructure by controlling many different autonomous systems within the city, such as energy consumption or public transport. Because RL algorithms are always learning and adapting to different scenarios, they can allow for more efficient resource use.

We've seen how AI algorithms and ML interplay and how important they are for the future of AI in diverse applications. There are three main types of ML: supervised, unsupervised, and reinforcement learning, and all of them have different applications when it comes to enabling ML and how they deal with experiences and data. When looking at supervised learning, this is extremely important when dealing with labeled data because it allows the AI to make accurate decisions and classifications.

So, with this type, we can use it in applications such as medical diagnosis or stock price prediction. Unsupervised learning is often used when we are dealing with unlabeled data, and it has its primary applications in clustering and anomaly detection. It also has many real-world applications, such as in recommendation systems. Lastly, RL allows AI to learn through trial and error, reward, and penalties, much like people do in certain circumstances. It has as many applications as we've seen, such as training autonomous vehicles or building an AI that can compete with real players in video games.

A real-life example of unsupervised learning would be the use of marketing analysis by a retail company that has a large customer base. Through unsupervised learning techniques, the company would be able to use tools such as clustering to group customers based on some of their shared characteristics, like preferences or demographics. When this identification is done, the business can tailor marketing strategies to each group of customers to make their marketing more effective.

In the next chapter, we will dive into the symbiotic relationship between data and AI. We are going to look at how data is collected and preprocessed, how to introduce big data and its impact on AI applications, and ethical data usage in AI.

3

DATA AND AI—A SYMBIOTIC RELATIONSHIP

It's estimated that in the past 2 years, there has been more data created than in the entire history of humanity before that (FLR Spectron, 2021). This is due to how fast we can generate data because of our computers, phones, and any other devices.

This is part of what we are going to explore in this chapter, along with the symbiotic relationship between this data and AI.

THE ROLE OF DATA IN AI

In this section, we will focus on how data is collected and its preprocessing, which means the cleaning, transforming, and integration of data in order to make it suitable for analysis. Essentially, this allows for an improvement in data quality and better outcomes when analyzing this data. We will also look into the correlation between big data and AI and ethical data usage in AI.

So, how is data collected? What are the main methods, and what are the challenges? Essentially, data acquisition is the process of acquiring raw data from the many sources available and creating datasets that are then used for analysis by AI. The quantity and quality of these datasets are essential when it comes to how successful AI projects as well as ML projects become.

There are several methods of data acquisition too, and each depends on the type of AI or the type of data in general. One of the first methods of data acquisition was manual data entry, which is still used today but is not the most prevalent method. As the name indicates, the data is added by a person or a team of people and is often used in small projects. It's extremely time-consuming and prone to mistakes, so it's not often used when there are large datasets.

Web scraping is another method to acquire data, and here, the data is taken from websites with specialized tools that allow the acquisition of this data or through the use of programming scripts. Crowdsourcing is yet another method often used, especially on crowdsourcing platforms, where individuals or groups of individuals can outsource and collect the data. There's also the purchase of data, which happens when companies purchase this data from third parties. These can include data that is specific to certain industries or market research. Sensor data collection is when devices and other sensors collect data from the real world, such as wearable devices like smartwatches, environmental sensors, or even GPS devices.

There are also challenges to data collection, such as data quality, that I've mentioned before. In order to ensure the accuracy of data, it's vital that the quality of this be excellent, or it can lead to inaccurate results. An example of low-quality data is biased data, which often leads to biased models. There's also the issue of ethics and data privacy, where the collection of this data has to be performed ethically. Data volume and variety can also be challenges when collecting them.

Where there are large volumes of data, it can be a problem to store it because it can drain resources and even the infrastructure. For this reason, the organization has to have good data management systems. The variety of data can also become a problem because data can come in many different formats, such as video, text, audio, or images. This means that handling all of this data might be a complex and sometimes time-consuming process.

The uniqueness of the data and its consistency can become a challenge because, when it comes to consistency, data might often come from different sources, which in itself might lead to inconsistencies, and integrating this data might be a little more complex. The uniqueness of the data refers to depicting a certain problem in an accurate way, which means that generic data might not be appropriate for training models in an effective way.

Data acquisition is necessary and vital when it comes to training AI projects, but its quantity and quality are also essential to making these projects work properly without inconsistencies or bias, which might have an impact on the outcomes.

The Importance of Data Preprocessing for Effective AI Models

As we've seen, data preprocessing is an essential step when acquiring data before it's fed into an AI, but how does the development of preprocessing go? What does the data go through before it can be used to train AI or come up with reliable outcomes?

First, there's the process of improving the data quality. When an organization acquires data, it is often raw, which means that it might contain errors such as missing values or inconsistencies. Processes such as data cleaning aid in the identification of these errors and improve the quality of the data. Normalization and scaling of data are also crucial processes in data preprocessing. This is done when the data acquired might have different ranges or scales, and so, through the process of normalization, whoever acquired the data is making sure that every single feature is standardized.

Often, in the preprocessing of data, there will be missing values, which might have consequences for the quality of the data and the training of AI. There are some techniques that can be used, such as imputation, which allows for the filling in of the missing values through estimation and comparison with the remaining data. Another technique used to improve data quality is feature engineering, which consists of choosing, changing, and creating new features from the new raw data. This allows AI systems to understand and get the most relevant information from the data they are fed.

Data transformation, in this context, essentially means that there's a need to form a linear relationship through data preprocessing to enhance the performance of the AI that uses such systems as linear regression.

There are other methods that can be used when preprocessing data, such as noise reduction. In this context, noise is related to inconsistencies or errors that are found in the data that might cause issues when the AI is trying to find patterns. This obviously might have an impact on the outcomes. There are methods such as filtering or smoothing that enhance data quality.

Noise can come from many sources, such as measurement errors, data entry errors, or, if data is collected from the real world, environmental factors that could be lightning changes or weather conditions. It's also important to note that preprocessing can significantly reduce computational power when training AI because it erases data that is not relevant, which leads to a reduction in resources needed and faster training times.

Exploring Data Cleaning and Feature Engineering

In this section, we will dive into two particular methods: data cleaning and feature engineering, because they are some of the most important in today's data processing. Let's start with data cleaning. This technique involves finding and fixing errors and other inaccuracies in the data received, and it's an important step in data preprocessing. Some of the most common techniques are data formatting, handling missing values, duplicate removal, and outlier detection. Data formatting consists of making sure the formatting of the data is consistent within a dataset, and every type of data should be in the same format, so AI can properly read it.

When it comes to handling missing values, as I've already mentioned, one of the best ways to tackle this issue is through imputation, which means adding the missing values. Another good technique used in data cleaning is outlier detection. This is done by understanding and identifying outliers using certain methods, such as IQR, and deciding if they should be changed or completely removed. It's important to tackle outliers because they can distort analysis. Duplicate removal is yet another technique used in data cleaning, and it consists of erasing duplicate data or records to remove redundant information.

Feature engineering, as we've seen, consists of coming up with new features or changing the existing ones to make the data a better fit for AI or training models. This allows for an enhancement of the model's performance to understand relevant patterns. There are many different techniques. For example, discretization is when you convert continuous numerical features into categories to grab nonlinear links more efficiently.

Feature extraction is when important information is extracted from the raw data, which makes it easier for models to perform. Feature transformation happens when, as the name indicates, there's a transformation in the features using operations such as exponentiation, square root, or logarithms to make them more fit for models. Or one-hot encoding, which essentially converts variables in categories into binary to also enhance ML algorithms.

Data cleaning and feature engineering involve a great understanding of the data and the problem at hand, and both of these broad methods can improve the performance of AI and ML models. But it's important to understand the processes and know when to use each one.

BIG DATA AND AI

Big data is essentially complex and large datasets that are far from the capacity of common data processing and the tools usually used to acquire and analyze them. It is usually defined by the three Vs: volume, variety, and velocity. Let's break it down. Volume means the amount of data, and obviously, big data has large volumes of it. This data often comes from many different sources, such as sensors, social media, or finances. Variety refers to how diverse big data is because it can come in many different formats, and to process all of these formats, you need flexible data processing procedures. Lastly, velocity refers to how fast this data is generated, which also requires fast processes to analyze it.

We can go a little further and add two more Vs that are often associated with big data: variability, which refers to inconsistency in formats, and in turn, adds complexity, and veracity, which is the uncertainty of the quality of the data (this is one of the reasons it's so important for this data to be preprocessed).

Big data is extremely significant for AI applications for a number of reasons. As we've seen, big data is important for model training to be able to come up with all sorts of scenarios when analyzing real-world data and have accurate outcomes. The more preprocessed data fed into AI applications, the more accurate it becomes, and the more accurate AI models can be when it comes to outcomes. This way, AI can find complex relationships that lead to better results. This also allows for much better insights that might not be possible to analyze with smaller datasets.

One of the most important aspects of big data has to do with NLPs, especially when training the AIs to understand and create text that is similar to what humans would create. Another important aspect of big data is in the healthcare sector and how it allows for training models to become more accurate at diagnosing diseases as well as finding new treatments. Autonomous systems, such as driverless cars, need to be fed big data, so they can come up with the best solutions when performing the task of driving.

In other words, big data is essential to powering modern AI applications and allowing them to be as sophisticated as possible. Data will continue to increase, which will allow AI models to become better at predicting, diagnosing, and coming up with more accurate outcomes for the most diverse scenarios. That's why people say that there's a symbiosis between big data and AI applications because, without it, we wouldn't have AI as we know it.

How Do AI Technologies Handle Large-Scale Data Analysis?

AI uses many different methods and techniques when it comes to handling big data analysis to achieve great results from large datasets. Let's see some of those methods.

I've already talked about some of those methods previously, such as data preprocessing, feature engineering, and ML algorithms, but there are many more. For example, they need specialized storage solutions to store the data and be able to manage it properly. Cloud-based store platforms are one of the best solutions for it because they allow scalability and great organization of datasets that keep growing. Distributed computing is a technique used to process and analyze data in many different places, and this data is often stored in clusters of computers, which allows the use of parallel processing.

Now, parallel processing is an AI framework designed to leverage distributed systems, like clusters of computers, and allow for the division of tasks throughout the network and processing them at the same time. This way, AI can reduce the processing time and analysis of this data. Speaking of processing, there are many different types besides parallel processing.

For example, stream processing is used for real-time data and allows the process to occur as it is generated, allowing AI to react to events right away. Batch processing is another processing method where data that is being analyzed is placed in batches. This method is quite effective for nonreal-time analysis, but it is also quite effective when it comes to the speed of processing these datasets.

Another method applied is dimensionality reduction, which is often used to reduce the number of features while maintaining the quality of the data. This is because large datasets can have many features, which might lead to a decrease in the accuracy of outcomes, so by reducing features, it becomes easier and more efficient to analyze the data.

There are many other techniques, but these are the most commonly used when it comes to handling large-scale data in AI systems. Often, many of these methods are combined to make the processing of data more efficient.

Cloud Computing and Big Data

I want to emphasize the role of cloud computing in handling big data because it has a massive impact on how AI systems operate today. The major change here is that cloud computing allows for a scalable infrastructure, especially when it comes to processing and storage capabilities. Cloud platforms allow for on-demand scalability, which in turn allows companies and other organizations to scale their resources based on the volume of data they have. This is vital for unexpected workloads, which, in fact, can happen quite a lot when dealing with big data.

Cloud platforms also provide many different storage options that are tailored for the organization using them. Here, some of the biggest platforms are Google Cloud Storage or Amazon S3. When it comes to data processing, cloud computing also plays a big role in providing managed services for data analysis or processing.

This type of computing is very cost-effective because it allows these companies and organizations to pay according to their usage, which is great when it comes to scalability. Cloud platforms also allow for global accessibility, so teams within different organizations can work and access data from anywhere in the world. It's also relevant to note that the security and compliance of these services are quite robust to ensure big data and AI systems are within industry regulations and data protection. Another great service that cloud computing offers is data integration, which essentially allows for easier integration of data from different sources.

So, as you can see, without cloud computing, we wouldn't have the AI systems that we currently have, and they provide an essential infrastructure for AI applications. It allows companies to leverage the power of big data without having to manage the data themselves and, at the same time, accelerate the processing of AI systems.

ETHICAL DATA USAGE IN AI

In this section, we will discuss ethical data usage in AI systems. We will highlight the concerns related to data privacy and bias in AI algorithms, the importance of transparency and fairness in AI decision-making, and discuss AI's potential for society and the need for responsible AI practices.

Starting with the concerns related to data privacy and bias in AI, these are vital to address if we are to enjoy the opportunities AI has given us as a society and ensure that AI develops. I will also highlight some of the strategies that can be used to mitigate these concerns. Starting with data privacy, one of the most common concerns voiced is data breaches. This often comes from a lack of security where this data is stored, which exposes sensitive information.

The only feasible way to prevent this is by implementing better security measures and having more regular security audits. This often involves the encryption of data, both in transit and stored, as well as the implementation of end-to-end encryption in communication channels. Improving the security of the network is also a good solution, such as implementing intrusion prevention and detection systems, or firewalls. Another way to prevent data breaches is through employee training and awareness.

Another concern when it comes to privacy is informed consent. This is a violation if collecting data requires prior consent from individuals. I'll give you a real-life example of improper informed consent in collecting data.

In 2021, WhatsApp, which is owned by Facebook, updated its privacy policy to allow information to be shared with Facebook, but in the privacy policy, they misled their users. While the update only focused on data sharing with business accounts, many believed their personal information was being shared on Facebook, which led to a massive backlash on the platform. With this, I'm trying to explain that companies should always be as transparent as possible when it comes to data collection and obtain consent at all times.

Data ownership and control are also issues that are often raised. Essentially, I think everyone can agree that people should have full control of their personal data and be informed about how others use it. However, this is not always the case, and to mitigate this issue, companies should have mechanisms in place for individuals to be able to change or delete their data as they please.

When it comes to bias in AI algorithms, we've seen that it comes from data, but it constitutes a massive issue because it prevents AI systems from producing accurate outcomes. Essentially, biased data leads to biased AI systems. And so, the only way we have today is to properly curate data to be diverse. Implementing fairness metrics to assess bias in AI systems will also ensure that decisions and other AI outcomes are unbiased.

The implementation of ethical guidelines should also be something that companies should be introducing (and some are) to address bias in the development of AIs. Of course, there are other things that can be done when it comes to bias in AI, such as human oversight, ongoing monitoring, and bias reporting channels for users to report instances of discrimination or bias in AI systems.

There's an urgent need to address these ethical concerns, but this requires AI developers and policymakers to work together to develop AIs that are transparent and unbiased, foster trust, and make sure the benefits AI brings are fair and just across different populations.

Importance of Transparency and Fairness in AI Decision-Making

Transparency and fairness are vital concepts when it comes to decision-making in AI, not only to give accurate results but also to ensure ethical AI systems. We've already talked about avoiding bias and discrimination, so I'm not going to elaborate much here, but it's one of the most important factors. Transparency and fairness are also important for trust and accountability, so users can understand how decisions made by AI systems are made. This means that the way AI systems work needs to be as transparent as possible. If this is done, it's a lot easier to hold AI developers accountable for outcomes that might not be as fair. Having accountability allows for trust in the systems and better adoption of AI across different sectors and in society.

Transparency is intrinsically related to the next point, explainability, which consists of providing explanations for AI decisions and allowing users to understand the reasoning behind a specific outcome. This is extremely important in a few sectors, such as finance or the healthcare industry, where a lack of explainability might have real-world consequences. A transparent and fair AI will also allow organizations that own the AI systems to comply with regulations and avoid any legal problems. This is even more important for businesses when it comes to maintaining their reputation. Businesses that prioritize fairness and transparency in AI systems not only maintain their reputation but also increase it in their industries.

The need for fairness and transparency when it comes to AI decisions requires a combined effort not only from developers but also a commitment from the organization. By doing this, it will not only be beneficial to users but also for the organizations that own those AI systems.

The Need for Responsible AI Practices and the Potential Impact on Society

AI has great potential to change many aspects of our society and, in fact, is already doing so. We can see it in transportation, healthcare, or even education. But with all this power comes a lot of responsibility, especially when it comes to ethical issues, as we've seen. This is the reason we need responsible AI practices that go along with the revolution that is already taking place. Let's discuss why responsible AI practices are essential.

For once, the ethical concerns we've already talked about. Every decision made through an AI system has to align with ethical principles and to have responsible AI practices, we need to make sure AI system outcomes are aligned with what we, as humans, consider ethically good, such as the promotion of fairness or avoiding biases. We've also mentioned fairness, transparency, and accountability, which are part of responsible AI practices. But when it comes to its potential impact on society, job displacement and its potential to have an impact on the economy are just as relevant.

AI, as well as automation through AI, can (and, in some cases, already has) disrupt the job market and whole sectors. There have to be strategies put in place to train workers, whether it is to reskill them and be able to work with AI systems or adapt their work to new functions, to make sure unemployment doesn't increase and impact the economy in a negative way. We can look at another solution here that consists of human-AI collaboration to mitigate job loss. With this, I mean that AI systems should be designed to work collaboratively with workers to reach better outcomes, instead of completely replacing them.

Environmental impact is yet another issue where there's a need for responsible AI practices. Here, we need to look at AI's computing power and what that means for energy consumption, which in turn leads us to these environmental issues. Here, we should be looking at ways to develop energy-efficient systems to mitigate these environmental issues. I can't talk about responsible AI practices without mentioning the legal and regulatory challenges AI has been going through. AI is evolving fast, but regulations and other laws regarding the issue are not keeping up with the pace at which these regulatory challenges develop.

There has to be better and faster work from policymakers when it comes to establishing regulations, so AI systems can be deployed safely. However, this also requires global collaboration from all countries. AI is not just local; it's spreading across the world, and we need organizations and countries to team up to establish universal guidelines when it comes to AI safety and ethics. AI's potential can completely change society as we know it, but with such a shift comes a lot of responsibility. We need to do better to ensure that AI continues to evolve while society remains safe.

The symbiotic relationship between data and AI systems is crucial, as we've seen and explored, one can't function without the other. The unprecedented creation of data in the last few years is intrinsically connected with the explosion of the AI and ML sectors. But this boom was initiated by the many devices we depend on in our daily lives, such as smartphones, computers, or any other device we use. However, having data and large volumes of it is not enough; we need to collect it at great speed and preprocess it before it is fed to AI systems. We've seen how data acquisition processes work and how the conversion of raw data into quality data is done. We've also seen what the current challenges are when it comes to all of these processes.

We've explored how all this data can be dangerous for society if we don't put ethical and safety regulations in place. It's extremely important to place ethical practices in our regulations and make them universal so everyone complies with them and users don't have their personal data spread across the internet without their consent. So, while the symbiotic relationship between data and AI is the most important thing when it comes to the development of AI systems, it's just as important to safeguard our society and our people through regulations and collaborations to ensure AI outcomes are ethical and have what it takes to continue to develop and make our lives easier.

4

THE POWER OF NEURAL NETWORKS

We can think of neural networks as an orchestra. In the same way that an orchestra is composed of many different instruments that contribute to the same output, a neural network is composed of many interconnected neurons that collaborate in many different ways to reach the same outcome.

This is exactly what we will be talking about in this chapter as we delve into the power of neural networks. We will explore what the definition of a neural network is, how these are trained, and the different types there are. Let's start with the basics.

ANATOMY OF A NEURAL NETWORK

As we've seen, neural networks are an essential piece of the puzzle that is AI and ML. They are based on our own brains, and their goal is to come up with different solutions for different problems. Let's take a look at the basic structure of a neural network. First, we have the layers, which we can divide into three: the input, hidden, and output layers. Layers are at the core of the neural network, and here we can find the connected nodes or neurons.

The input layer is where data goes in and is the first layer "touched" by data. Here, the nodes answer to the different characteristics of the data. The hidden layers are between the input layers and the output layers, and their function is to shift the input data. Lastly, the output layer creates what we see: the output. Then, there are nodes, which are processing units, and regardless of the layer they are in, they all have the ability to receive data and create outcomes.

What Are the Activation Functions in Signal Propagation?

The role of activation functions in the signal propagation of neural networks is crucial because they allow the AI or ML system to understand complex relationships, which leads to better outcomes. This is mainly accomplished because they introduce nonlinearity to the network. But you might be wondering what exactly activation functions are in signal propagation. Essentially, if you are making a cake, you need certain ingredients such as eggs, flour, and sugar, and each of these ingredients is needed for the cake. However, there might be times when you need to add something extra to make the cake good.

If we grab this analogy, the AI is the chef trying to bake the cake, and the different ingredients are the signals received by the AI. But, just as a baker would need to understand how important each ingredient is for the cake, so does an AI system need to know the importance of each signal before coming up with the outcome. Much like a chef trying to understand what ingredient he would have to add more of just by trying the mix, the activation function of the AI is the same. They go by trial and error and "taste" the mix, trying to find the right balance.

So, if the system understands that one of the signals is more important than another, it will use more of that one, as if a chef would realize that sugar is more important than eggs when baking a cake. The activation function allows the system to understand what is important and helps them decide how much of each signal they should give more importance to.

In a neural network, the different nodes receive input signals from other nodes in the previous layer (so if the output signal came from the input layer, this would be received by the nodes in the hidden layer). Then, these signals will go through the activation function to attribute the importance of each signal and to find out the output of the nodes that will be sent to the next layer (which, if we are following the example above, would be the output layer). But, how is this important for signal propagation?

Well, for one, the introduction of nonlinearity, as I've mentioned, allows for more complex problem-solving and identifying more complex patterns. But, it also allows the systems to learn more complex features and enhance expressiveness. So, as we can see, activation functions are essential for neural networks because they allow them to understand more complex patterns and learn more complex features that have an impact on the system's outcomes.

I want to discuss the concepts of weights and biases in neural networks, and I will continue with the cake analogy used above. If you are a baker, and you're teaching someone how to bake cakes, you would usually give them a basic recipe, even though every cake is different. Because of that, even if you give them a basic recipe, you have to teach them the little tweaks each recipe has. With neural networks, we can look at nodes as the newcomer that you're trying to teach how to bake, and the little adjustments in the recipe are the weights and biases.

Let's start with weights, and in our analogy, that would be the relevance attributed to each ingredient in the recipe. Sometimes, we use more of one ingredient than another, depending on the recipe. In neural networks, nodes have a certain weight linked to them, and those weights serve to determine how much influence that specific node will have on the output of the system. When it comes to biases, we have to go back to the cake analogy and picture that when adjusting the recipe, there's a preference for how the cake will taste.

This is like a bias, and it's where adjustments start because it's the foundation of how to change it. If you know that you want a cake that is sweeter, then the bias will go more toward sweetness. In neural networks, there are biases that can be seen as starting points that determine how much the nodes should activate even before anything happens. So, the weight determines the importance of inputs, and biases determine the likelihood of a node activating. Then, considering all of this, there are adjustments to these two parameters that happen during the training of the system to have better outcomes. In other words, weights and biases are fundamental for the tuning of the outcomes of AI systems.

TRAINING NEURAL NETWORKS

In this section, we will explore slightly different processes when it comes to training neural networks, such as backpropagation for adjusting weights during training, the use of gradient descent when optimizing performance, and the importance of hyperparameter tuning when it comes to achieving better outcomes.

Let's start with backpropagation. This is an essential concept when it comes to training neural networks, and we can look at it as a feedback loop that aids the network in not only learning but also improving its performance over long periods. I'll use another analogy here to try to make sense of how the process works. If you're learning how to play the guitar, you are likely to start by learning a simple song and to understand how good you are at it, you listen to the recording of what you just played.

Here, you can understand where the mistakes are; there might be timing issues, wrong notes, or many other things. But, now that you know where to improve, you continue your practice, focusing on overcoming the issues you had in your recording. Then, you continue with the same process: train, record, understand the mistakes, and practice again in a loop. This is not different from what happens with the backpropagation process in neural networks, although they use different names.

For instance, a forward pass is when the network receives input, processes it through its layers, and tries to produce the outcome, just as you'd play the guitar. Then, you'd go into the comparison stage, where you compare the output of the system with what it is supposed to be, just as when you listen to your own recording. Here, the neural network would compare the mistakes it had made.

Then, there's the backward pass stage, and here is where the actual backpropagation happens. Here, the neural network would identify the mistakes made and adjust to solve the issues, and this is where the weights and biases are adjusted. This happens by looking at things backward, going through the layers, and shifting things based on the mistakes it made. When doing this, just as you'd learn from your mistakes while playing the guitar, so would the neural network, which allows it to improve.

Here, there's an important algorithm at play that I will discuss later in more detail, but it's important to highlight it here too, called gradient descent. This is an optimization algorithm that decreases the mistakes made gradually and helps find the perfect values for the biases and weights that do just that. The network continues to do so, and it becomes better and better each time. The backpropagation process means many rounds of forward passing, comparison, and backpropagation to adjust weights and biases until the neural network is able to come up with accurate outcomes.

Let's now explore how gradient descent works since it's such an important process of backpropagating. We can look at this as a vital optimization tool when training neural networks. The main goal here is to adjust the different parameters, such as weights and biases, so it begins at the initial point, which is the weights and biases, then goes from top to bottom to try and update the parameters that might have been wrong before. However, this is usually controlled by something called the learning rate, which helps determine how big the update has to be. You can look at this as someone going down a steep mountain, and each and every step is an adjustment to the parameters until you get to the bottom.

But there's another technique used when it comes to achieving better outcomes and optimizing the performance of neural networks, and it's called hyperparameter tuning. As the name indicates, it helps with fine-tuning parameters after training; however, these are often set before training even begins. As you can imagine, this has a big impact on neural networks because it helps determine how a system learns from the data received after training and how it connects with data that has never been seen before. But unlike gradient descent, which shifts weight and bias, hyperparameter tuning shifts overfitting and underfitting.

Overfitting often happens when the system is too complex and captures things that don't matter, such as noise in training data, and underfitting is the opposite when the model is far too simple to even identify any patterns or relevant data to make a prediction. When hyperparameter tuning is done right, it can really optimize the system. However, hyperparameter tuning is very important for gradient descent because it allows it to find the optimal learning rate, which in turn makes training go much faster. In sum, hyperparameter tuning is an important technique that defines how fast a system can learn during training.

TYPES OF NEURAL NETWORKS

Even though we've talked about neural networks, we haven't talked about the different types there are, and this is exactly what we will be talking about here. We will also explore what they are used for and their roles in different processes.

There are many different types, so I'm just going to mention some of the most common ones. For example, the feedforward neural network is one of the most basic types of neural networks, and here data moves only in one direction. In this case, from input layers to hidden layers and finally to output layers. This type of neural network is often used for things like classification.

There's also the recurrent neural network (RNN), that is used in tasks such as sequential data, such as text, for instance. These don't move only in one direction and can loop back because they have memory of previous inputs. Here, most language models are based on RNN. Another common neural network is the convolutional neural network (CNN), which is often tasked with image recognition and other tasks such as processing. They are often used in this field because they can quickly identify visual data.

Again, there are many more, but these are the important ones to continue our discussion, where I will talk about the applications of convolutional neural networks in image recognition. It's relevant to talk about these because they revolutionized the sector of image recognition as well as computer vision. This is often due to their capacity to quickly understand and capture certain features in images. When it comes to applications, there are many already in use. For instance, face recognition is one of them. CNNs are often used for facial recognition systems because they are extremely efficient at identifying features —in this case, facial features that are used for identity verification.

Another great application of CNNs is object identification, where these neural networks can identify an object in a whole image, which is extremely important for things like autonomous vehicles, especially when it comes to identifying traffic signs or pedestrians crossing the road. Another application is image classification, where CNNs can simply classify and identify animals and objects, or even understand and identify diseases from medical imaging.

This is why CNNs were so important in the image recognition field and will continue to be so because of the potential they can bring to the most diverse fields.

I would also like to highlight the role of RNN in sequential data processing and why it's so relevant. The main characteristic of this neural network is the fact that it has an internal memory, so to speak, that helps it handle sequences because it knows important data from previous steps that has an influence on future outcomes. The applications of this are numerous, such as in NLP or speech recognition. But, let's look at how RNN works.

When trying to come up with real-world scenarios and predictions, we know that many of the data points are sequential or temporal; for example, looking at NLPs, we know that depending on the context, a single word might have different meanings. And this context depends on the words that came before it. This is also useful for predicting the weather, stock prices, or anything where the present might be influenced by the past.

Another important feature of RNNs is shared weights, which simply means that the weights that we've been talking about in the previous sections are shared across other steps. This feature allows the RNN to understand patterns better, especially in sequential data, simply by retaining information from other steps in the past. Not only are RNNs great at language modeling, translation, or speech recognition, but they are also used in video analysis, healthcare, or even music generation.

The neural network sector is very interesting and has tremendous potential in our society. We've looked at how training processes are done, the types of neural networks, and the many applications they have. Neural networks are very similar to how the human brain works, and much like our brain, they can leverage the connections between neurons to come up with solutions to the most varied challenges. As you know, neural networks are composed of layers, which in this particular case represent the stages of processing information and finding outcomes.

We've also talked about the concept of activation functions and their ability to perform nonlinear functions that allow these neural networks to understand complex patterns and relationships. We've also seen how weights and biases work within a neural network and how these have an impact on how much the neural network distributes the importance of the input signals.

With this, the neural networks have the ability to adjust their outcomes during training to fine-tune and have more accurate predictions and outcomes. Another concept that we've looked at is backpropagation, where a neural network is able to understand the mistakes made and optimize its outputs, akin to trial and error.

We've also explored the different neural networks, such as CNN or RNN, and their different applications in the real world. We can conclude that there's a large array of applications for different neural networks just by analyzing a small fraction of them. All of this has a tremendous impact on both AI and ML, and it will continue to evolve as AI developers continue to find new ways of training these systems, and with that, more applications will come.

5

AI IN EVERYDAY LIFE

Picture the daily routine of a teacher, which usually involves coming up with lessons, grading tests, and teaching kids. Regardless of how committed the teacher is to their job, there's a lot of work to do, which leaves almost no room for more personalized attention to their students. However, the teacher starts playing with an AI-powered educational platform, and one day, she decides to give it a try. One week goes by, and the AI system starts to analyze how the students behave and their overall performance. This allows the system to understand what topics students tend to struggle with and what topics they are better at.

During a math lesson, the system finds out that some students are struggling to grasp a concept, but the teacher doesn't catch it. However, the system alerts the teacher that instead of moving on with the material, it suggests that the teacher try another way of conveying that particular concept. And so, the teacher does it, and it works, and the students understand the concepts.

The more time the system spends analyzing the students, the more and better insights it can come up with, and it can even create personalized tasks and exercises for specific students. With this, the teacher spends less time on the different ways to come up with a clear explanation of some topics and more time interacting with the students.

This introduction of the AI system into the classroom completely transformed the dynamics of how the teacher presented the material and helped her understand better how to convey some of the information while having more time to interact with the students.

In this chapter, we will look at AI in everyday life and how it can help us, much like it helped the teacher in the example above. We will divide this chapter into the three main areas where AI influences our daily lives: NLP, smart homes, and healthcare.

UNDERSTANDING NLP

NLP allows AI to understand and process human language, but how exactly does it do it? Through AI systems, NLP can analyze text and gain important insights from it. Essentially, the algorithms behind NLPs are created to understand the context, structure, and semantics of the human language, and with this information, they can understand meanings in the text as well as identify places, objects, individuals, and more. NLP can also break down the information into smaller bits called tokens (usually sentences or words), which allows the system to analyze the whole text more consistently.

The system can also understand and identify entities such as people within the text, which allows it to understand and formulate results; this is a process called entity recognition. NLPs can also understand and analyze sentiment to find out the emotional tone in the text given, which might not particularly be good for something like ChatGPT, but it's crucial for NLPs that try to decipher social media sentiment. NLPs are also great at translation and can do this almost instantly, as well as question answering, which is great for chatbots. But one of the most impressive processes of NLP is text generation, such as ChatGPT, which can create human-like text just through a small prompt.

NLP closes the gap between human and machine language and allows it to interact with people. As we've seen, it has numerous applications and will continue to do so as it keeps evolving. Let's now look at the importance of sentiment analysis and speech recognition within NLPs.

We've briefly talked about it, but these are two fundamental concepts of NLP that have many different applications in many different industries. Let's start with sentiment analysis. As I've said previously, through sentiment analysis, AI can understand human emotions, usually through the emotional tone in texts. There are usually three states: neutral, positive, and negative, and understanding the sentiment of feedback, reviews, or social media posts, often used by businesses, allows insights from their customers. Let's delve into this a little further.

For example, sentiment analysis is very important for brand reputation management, where NLPs can monitor sentiment across many platforms, such as social media, and give insights into the business and suggestions on how to handle the brand's reputation. It's also useful for customer experience and how to manage it. Businesses are able to track the sentiment of their customers and identify areas where they can improve. It's also great for product development or market research, where sentiment analysis can be crucial to finding out about emerging patterns or market trends and knowing how to make decisions based on them.

When it comes to speech recognition, NLPs also have many applications that can be important. One of these is accessibility. Speech recognition technology helps people with disabilities and allows them to use devices that they would otherwise not use. Speech recognition can also make workflow more effective because it streamlines it. For instance, instead of writing a text, you can simply dictate it while taking important notes. It's also important for language translation, especially in real time when trying to have a conversation with people who don't speak the same language.

There are many other important aspects of NLP, but these are perhaps the most relevant. By only looking at speech recognition and sentiment analysis, we can clearly see how powerful NLP is and the potential it can have in the near future. Let's look at some real-life examples of NLP-powered applications.

Virtual personal assistance started to become quite popular in the last few years, especially with Alexa, Google Assistant, and Siri, and all of these devices use NLP to understand what is said and to respond. Customer chatbots are also very popular, and many companies that deal with customers use them nowadays. They are able to answer queries and triage customers to the specific customer service department. Email filtering, resume screening, fraud detection, and speech-to-text transcription are also some other uses of real-life NLPs that many businesses and individuals use today.

AI IN SMART HOMES AND THE INTERNET OF THINGS

AI use in smart homes and on the Internet of Things (IoT) has seen tremendous advances over the years. Before we get into it, I'll just explain what IoT means. This often refers to a network of physical devices (the things) that have something that allows them to connect to the internet or other devices and have the capability of sending and receiving data.

This can be any device, such as a car, a phone, machinery, or any other thing that you might think of that is capable of that. However, to be considered devices belonging to the IoT, these usually don't need someone to actively send or exchange information; they can do it on their own. Some of the things that belong to the IoT might have the ability to collect and share data; they might be able to perform any sort of automation; they might have sensors; or they might have remote monitoring. Now that you understand that, let's first talk about smart homes and how AI allows for automation and connectivity with them.

As you know, smart homes are becoming increasingly popular, and AI has a tremendous role in all of them, especially in automation and connectivity, where the ultimate goal is to create a living environment for people inside their own homes. Here's how these two parameters play out with AI: Smart homes have sensors; in most cases, smart devices within the household have these, which allow for the collection of data about the behavior of the people living there and many other things. AI is able to analyze all the data that comes from the sensors of the smart home and understand patterns and other trends.

One of the most common examples is the temperature of the house, with the thermostat being controlled by AI, following the resident's preferences, and also being able to adjust it as it sees fit. Smart homes also have great device integration and connectivity. There are many different devices spread around the house that are able to collect the most varied data; besides the thermostat, there are usually security cameras, lights, and other appliances. The

AI systems embedded in the house can connect all of these, and with that, devices are able to communicate with one another and collaborate to create the environment of the house.

Any automation the smart home does comes from the data collected by its devices and sensors, which allows it to predict outcomes based on that information with a certain autonomy. Based on the resident's daily routines, weather, or even time of day, the smart home can adjust temperature, lighting, and anything else. Of course, there are also virtual assistants that the residents can simply communicate with, and the smart home responds to the command. Not only that, but some smart homes can also respond to gestures.

But one of the best features of smart homes is the use of AI to become more energy-efficient because they can control energy usage simply by analyzing the data received from the many devices spread across the house. You can even equip the smart home with security features such as facial recognition, for instance. But there's more that you can do, such as motion detection, or even the ability to recognize suspicious behavior if something is out of the ordinary, which in turn can send alerts to the residents or even the police.

Another great feature of smart homes is predictive maintenance, where the AI embedded in the smart home can monitor the performance of the different devices, understand when they might fail, and alert the residents beforehand. Of course, residents also have remote access to the smart home even when they are not in it, and this can usually be done through their phones or tablets. With that, they can manage the most diverse appliances around the house from afar.

Let's delve a little deeper into one of the best features of AI connectivity with smart homes, and how energy optimization and security actually work. Starting with energy optimization, we've seen that AI is able to collect and analyze data from connected devices, which includes resident behavior, appliance usage, and lightning usage. From here, the AI starts to understand trends and patterns, identify where energy is being wasted, and start to reduce it. Smart thermostats are one of the most common ways to reduce energy consumption, not just by learning the residents' habits but also by understanding when they are not home and when the heating or AC should be off.

Another important thing that I've mentioned above is the predictive analysis of AI when it comes to energy consumption, which comes from historical data collected and analyzed and allows it to adjust the settings of the temperature in every room. Better yet, AI can be coupled with renewable energy devices and appliances, such as solar panels, to understand energy generation from these and, with that, adjust itself as it receives more data.

The AI embedded in a smart home has the ability to understand what appliances are more energy-intensive, such as ovens or washing machines, and be able to schedule the starting of these at off-peak energy hours. As any AI would, it can give feedback and recommendations to the residents on how they can reduce energy consumption.

Now, when it comes to the security systems of a smart home, AI can be very helpful. We've already talked about facial recognition, which might be a great asset to keeping your home safe, but there are many other things. For instance, AI is able to understand and analyze behavior, in particular the behavior of residents, and so it is also able to distinguish standard behavior from suspicious behavior, and when something is off, it can send alerts to residents or even the police. This could be used in case an intruder gets inside the property, for instance. If an intruder is breaking in, or even if it's outside the house and security cameras capture it, they can send real-time alerts to the residents, so they can promptly respond and prevent anything from happening.

AI is already in many smart homes, and it's an upward trend, so we can expect to have more homes equipped with AI systems, which will improve energy consumption across countries, but it's also a great help when it comes to security and monitoring homes with the goal of increasing the resident's quality of life.

There are already many real-world examples of AI-powered IoT devices in the most diverse sectors. We've seen smart thermostats or smart cameras such as Ring Doorbell, for instance. But it already goes way beyond that. We are probably familiar with wearables usually linked to fitness and health, such as the Apple Watch or Fitbit, which are able to track a person's heart rate, sleep patterns, or any other type of physical activity and provide insights. When it comes to smart homes, appliances such as fridges are also becoming increasingly popular. For instance, the Samsung Family Hub Refrigerator can track the expiration dates of the food inside or suggest recipes with the food you have in the fridge.

Within the home, there are many others, such as smart lighting, smart pet feeders, or even smart locks. Outside the home, there have been some extraordinary advances, such as in agriculture with crop monitoring systems. These are capable of monitoring weather forecasts or soil conditions, which allows farmers to optimize their tasks such as pest control or fertilization. Even our cities are becoming smarter, and one of the first steps they are taking is incorporating smart traffic lights with real-time information to optimize signal timings with the goal of decreasing congestion.

AI IN HEALTHCARE AND MEDICINE

One of the most promising uses of AI is in healthcare and medicine, where it's already changing things for the better, especially when it comes to diagnosis and treatment. Because of AI's ability to analyze large volumes of data and understand patterns, it can also give better outcomes when it comes to the treatments used. Let's explore AI's potential in disease diagnosis and medical image analysis. Starting with the latter, there are three main branches where AI is advancing fast: ophthalmology, radiology, and histopathology.

In ophthalmology, AI is able to identify eye diseases by simply analyzing retinal images. Not only that, it can detect them prematurely, which allows time for an intervention that can save their vision. In radiology, it works similarly, with AI being able to analyze medical images such as CT scans or X-rays and identify anything that might be wrong much better than human medical professionals. In histology and pathology, AI can help medical professionals identify certain cellular pattern changes that might become more serious issues.

When it comes to the diagnosis and prediction of diseases, AI systems can predict the risk of cardiovascular diseases, for instance, but also many other disorders such as neurological disorders or cancer detection by analyzing patient data. This brings many benefits, such as early detection, which can literally save lives, but also comes up with personalized treatments for different patients by looking at their data and genetic information, which allows the patient to get the best possible treatment. This also has a positive influence on medical professionals by reducing their workload and automating repetitive tasks, which allows them to focus on other issues.

The Use of AI for Drug Discovery and Personalized Treatment Plans

AI has many other functions in healthcare, as we will see in this section, such as in drug discovery. Again, most of the leverage comes from how fast AI can analyze large amounts of data, which not only helps patients and medical professionals alike but also accelerates the process of finding new drugs, enhancing existing ones, or optimizing treatments. Let's focus on drug discovery first.

Here, AI targets understand biological data and find potential drug targets that might be linked to certain diseases. This allows for the acceleration of discovering drugs because researchers will know exactly where to look. Moreover, AI can simulate multiple scenarios between the new drug and patients to find out if there are any issues, which accelerates one of the most time-consuming processes when it comes to bringing new drugs onto the market. Not only that, AI can also predict how efficient a drug can be in different patients and find out the most effective treatment for them.

With all of this data, AI can personalize treatment plans by looking at drug and treatment data and patient data. This AI can predict how a patient will react to certain treatments by looking at a patient's medical records and coming up with personalized treatments. As you might imagine, this comes with many benefits, such as tailored interventions and the reduction of trial and error when it comes to drug design. It also allows for all of these processes to be much faster and more efficient.

Challenges and Ethical Considerations in AI-Driven Healthcare

There are a few challenges that we need to overcome before we can use the full potential of AI in the healthcare sector. Some of those are the same ethical challenges we have with AI in other sectors. Issues such as the privacy and security of patients' data, transparency, fairness, and bias, or informed consent. However, there are others. For example, one of the most talked about is the unexpected outcomes that AI might produce that could harm patients.

This means that AI might not always be able to anticipate negative consequences for patients, and so it requires constant monitoring from medical professionals. This leads us to the question: Who takes accountability if such negative consequences happen? There has to be a way to determine whose responsibility it is if there are AI-related mistakes in the diagnosis, for instance. Here, there have to be clear guidelines to know who is responsible for such mistakes.

Another challenge is the high cost of implementing AI systems and who gets to have them first. This is another ethical issue since, if we follow what society tends to do, those who have more money are the ones who will be able to enjoy AI's capability in the sector, which is unfair as everyone should be able to get the best possible treatment. Another issue plagues other sectors too: job displacement. If AI is adopted across the healthcare sector, this might have a negative impact on medical professionals. The solution is the same as in other sectors, such as providing training to the workers, so they can collaborate with AI and improve their AI skills.

Here, there's an urge to address these challenges probably more than in other sectors because we fully understand how beneficial the introduction of AI systems might be for people, but as with everything, things have to be done properly, and there needs to be a fair approach to ensure people's personal data is secured and that medical professionals don't lose job opportunities.

We've explored how AI is quickly integrating into the everyday lives of society through the most diverse neural networks, such as NLP, healthcare, and smart homes. As we've seen, NLP is crucial when it comes to allowing AI to understand not only human speech but also written text and even generate text. There are many applications for it, such as virtual assistants, which gather information for businesses when it comes to understanding their customers and what steps to follow to make their business more engaging. AI is also progressively being used in our homes, which allows for enhanced security and a decrease in energy usage, among many other things.

In healthcare, AI has the potential to revolutionize people's lives in ways that we were not capable of until now; from better diagnosis and analysis to personalized treatments or even new drug discoveries. However, there are a few challenges that we need to overcome until this is widely spread in the sector. In the following chapter, we will delve into what we can expect from AI in the near future in the most diverse sectors of society, from finance to transportation to even creativity.

6

THE FUTURE OF AI

"Artificial intelligence is not about replacing humans; it's about amplifying human potential. "
–Kai-Fu Lee

This has been the promise as we look into the future of AI, which we will be exploring in this chapter. There's fear of job displacement, but ultimately, AI's job is to enhance human capability and increase the quality of life in our society. Here, we will be looking at the future of AI in certain industries, such as the finance and banking industry, transportation and logistics, and the creative field.

AI IN FINANCE AND BANKING

AI has the potential to completely shift the finance and banking industries, as it is already doing at some level. However, the future is a lot more promising. As we've seen when we were looking at neural networks, AI can be of much help when it comes to fraud detection. Banks and other financial institutions have to deal with many different transactions on a daily basis, which makes it nearly impossible to verify any fraud if we only rely on workers. However, AI is here to change that with a fast analysis of financial data and an understanding of financial behaviors. As we've seen, anomaly detection and behavior analysis will shine in this regard.

But not only in fraud detection will the finance industry shift, but also in risk assessment. There are many AI-driven models regarding risk assessment already in use to allow banks and other financial institutions, as well as businesses, to identify their clients' eligibility for credit cards or loans. These AIs can analyze current clients' credit scores by looking at credit history and predicting the likelihood of a client defaulting on their loans. All of this is coupled with the fact that these analyses can be done in real time, which accounts for other factors such as economic conditions, market indicators, and many other factors.

Another area where AI is being used quite a lot is in trading, where systems can understand sentiment and market data and predict the price of certain stocks. But they can also have an overview of the market, which is important for market surveillance as well as anti-money laundering schemes. With this, AI systems can identify potential market manipulation or detect suspicious activities regarding money laundering. But let's have a better look at how AI algorithms work in trading.

These are often referred to as algorithm-trading (or algo-trading, for short) and are often used to make trades in the market. As I've pointed out, these systems can analyze market data and find trading opportunities, as well as make trades.

They work like many other AI systems in other sectors. They process market data such as trading volumes, sentiment, or price movements and try to find a pattern that might mean a great trading opportunity. Some of the techniques used by these AI systems are to look for price discrepancies, and when they find a variance, they make a trade to try and profit from it. There are also market-making systems, which I will not get into as deeply since they're not part of this book's topic, but market makers are essential to bringing liquidity into the market.

Essentially, if the market is not liquid, this means there's not enough money in the market, and people's trades might not give money back, which is an entirely new problem since there's a need to maintain liquidity in the market. However, the role of AI systems when it comes to market-making is for them to continue to make buy and sell orders, which maintains liquidity in the market.

They can also engage in high-frequency trading (HFT), which essentially means having the ability to make a larger number of orders at once based on real-time data. And, as you might know, timing is extremely important in the stock market. Another thing AI systems can do in the financial market is assessing risk. Here, algorithms can identify and manage risk by looking at data, understanding position sizes, and applying many other techniques that allow them to manage the risk of investments.

Although there are also some problems associated with AI entering the financial market, one of these is a technique that I've already mentioned: HFT. Because of how quickly these trades are made, this often contributes to market volatility. Because of this, regulatory bodies have to keep an eye on these AI systems to make sure market stability is there and to know if they are operating fairly. However, on the other hand, AI offers many benefits, such as the capability to analyze data a lot faster than a human could and an increase in efficiency and accuracy.

When it comes to the potential impact of AI in the future of the finance and banking sectors, looking at what is already in place, we can predict a big change. Just by looking at the methods we have today when it comes to data analysis and how fast AI systems can process large volumes of financial data in real time, they can allow people and financial institutions to become more informed on their investment decisions, predictions, and risk assessment, which leads to better strategies.

One important factor here is that the learning these AI systems are going through is continuous, so it's very plausible that they will become better and better at analyzing and coming up with more sophisticated strategies. This leads us to quantitative financial models that improve AI systems' abilities to identify more complex patterns in the data received, which can lead to more profitable trades.

It's also plausible that credit scoring will also become more sophisticated and new models will appear, which will make predictions more accurate and help people who might have been neglected by the current credit scoring method get a chance to borrow money. Another area of finance that AI will improve is financial inclusion, where AI is helping financial services be extended to people who are usually outside the financial system because of social or geographical reasons.

I have to talk about an AI application that was one of the first to be used in the sector, and that is robo-advisors. These AI-driven systems essentially trade assets based on the customer's risk assessment and necessities. With the advance of AI, we can see robo-advisors becoming increasingly important as well as more accurate.

AI IN TRANSPORTATION AND LOGISTICS

The transportation and logistics sectors have also gone through a massive transformation with the emergence of AI, which has enabled different ways for people and goods to move around the world. We live in a world where urban areas have exponentially increased, and so there's a constant flow of goods that are essential for society. This needs great transportation and logistics to keep up with the demand. Current systems have been struggling for a while to keep up the pace; however, the integration of AI came to solve many of the challenges the sectors were facing.

In this section, we will be discussing how AI transformed vehicles and helped manage traffic, as well as the role of AI in optimizing supply chains. Let's start with autonomous vehicles, which we've talked about briefly in other chapters. These types of vehicles would not be possible without the use of AI, but there are many benefits to autonomous vehicles, such as reducing traffic congestion and accidents, as well as mitigating emissions transmitted into the air. These vehicles, thanks to AI, have the ability to map and pinpoint the location of objects, which allows safe driving.

This is mostly due to the perception that vehicles, through cameras and sensors, are connected to AI. Here, these sensors send data to the AI system embedded in the vehicle, which then identifies other obstacles, such as other cars or pedestrians, as well as road signs. From here, and because AI can analyze data extremely fast, this allows these autonomous vehicles to make fast decisions considering the data fed by the sensors and cameras.

When it comes to traffic management, there are many changes that AI has brought and continues to bring that allow for smoother and more efficient transportation networks. For instance, AI can process real-time traffic analysis, which is fed by traffic cameras, GPS, or any other sensors on roads that allow it to monitor traffic congestion in real time. This not only allows drivers' autonomous vehicles or GPS to provide alternative ways, but in case of accidents, it alerts authorities much faster.

One of the best applications of AI in traffic management is traffic signal control, which has the ability to change signal timing based on traffic circumstances. This, in turn, makes it easier to reduce congestion. As you might know, because of AI's predictive analysis, it can also understand when congestion and accidents are more likely to happen, which allows for better traffic management and offers alternatives.

AI is also having a massive impact on optimizing supply chain operations, which allows for more accuracy and efficiency when it comes to trading goods across the world. AI systems have had an impact on almost every aspect of the supply chain, from production to distribution or even inventory management. Let's talk about how AI changed different aspects of the supply chain operation.

With inventory management, AI is able to understand the many different variables at play, such as demand fluctuations or lead times, and with that, avert under- or overstocking and enable cost savings. It also plays an important role in demand forecasting by looking at market trends, economic factors, or historical sales data to understand and optimize inventory levels.

They can also provide businesses with supplier management, which means that they can constantly assess the performance of the supplier but also identify factors outside the industry, such as economic or environmental factors, that might have an impact on the supply chain.

This allows businesses to make better decisions and identify potential risks.

When it comes to logistics or routing, AI also plays a big role by analyzing existing routes and optimizing those by looking at the different parameters that might condition these routings. For instance, these systems take into account traffic conditions or weather conditions to reduce delivery times and decrease transportation costs. They also play an important role in risk management and assessment, such as supplier disruption or market volatility, and in coming up with contingency plans to mitigate any potential issues.

AI can also assist businesses in designing better supply chain networks by analyzing different parameters such as customer locations, overall cost, and understanding the most efficient warehouses or transportation routes. Incorporating AI in transportation and logistics really made the industry advance, especially if we consider that it has been struggling to keep up with demand as the world's population continues to grow. But AI in this sector is still quite new, and it requires businesses to come up with great approaches to incorporate the technology and become more adaptable.

I've already given some examples of real-world examples of AI-driven transportation solutions like self-driving vehicles or smart traffic lights, but there are a few other examples, and it's very likely that we will be seeing a lot more of these over the years. For example, Los Angeles and Singapore implemented AI-powered traffic management systems that use different data sources, from cameras to mobile phones, to identify traffic patterns, anticipate traffic congestion, or provide better routes to drivers. But it can go further than that, as AI can also predict maintenance for vehicles, although so far only for those that have AI predictive maintenance systems.

They can monitor the current condition of these vehicles and alert the drivers when the vehicle should go in for inspection or maintenance. Not only on the ground, as seen with advances in vehicles, but also in the air with air traffic control management. Here, AI works alongside airports to optimize air traffic routes. For instance, the FAA in the US uses AI systems to help them with that.

When it comes to public transport, cities like Helsinki in Finland have incorporated AI-driven public transit systems to optimize schedules and routes, which allows for an increase in efficiency in the whole public transportation system. These are just some examples, but the AI applications in transport solutions go far beyond that already, and it's very likely that more and more applications will happen as AI gets better.

AI AND CREATIVITY

AI has a lot of potential in the most diverse fields, such as the arts and music, and it was one of the first industries where AI became established. Even though the creative field is often associated with human emotion, AI still has a role to play in it, and it mostly assists or amplifies human creativity. Let's take a look at how AI is combined in these fields. Some AI systems are coded to compose music by analyzing many different songs and coming up with melodies and rhythms.

While there's still a lot of improvement to be made in this particular aspect of music, AI can already imitate some styles of composers in the music it creates. However, the most used aspect of AI is in the creation of artwork, and there are many different applications there, such as Midjourney, where AI systems can mimic many different artistic styles and create art pieces through a small prompt written by people.

But it's in virtual reality and augmented reality that AI has the highest potential because it allows for the enhancement of the experience by creating realistic environments. In general design and visual effects, there are also some applications for AI where the systems can improve images and are amply used in video games and the film industry.

There are other aspects where AI can be useful besides creating things; for example, in conservation and restoration, where AI plays a crucial role when it comes to preserving art pieces. The system can analyze the original art from an image or picture and fix damages. But, as I've pointed out earlier, AI can also help with the recommendation and curation of TV shows, movies, or music by analyzing users' behaviors and recommending what to watch or listen to next, which increases their engagement.

However, AI has also been having some challenges. In fact, recently, there has been a particular case that has been highly debated that had to do with plagiarism used by services such as Midjourney when it came to mimicking the style of real artists. This is because AI takes from the original artist and creates something that is similar or, at times, even reproduces work that already exists. This brings up the issue of infringement of intellectual property rights.

Another challenge has to do with determining authorship and attributing the work to someone. This is because when AI creates art in any form, who is credited with the work? Is it the algorithm, the programmer, or the artist that inspired that art? This is vital to ensure all parties are recognized properly for the work.

However, one of the biggest issues has to do with the loss of human craftsmanship and the erosion of cultural identity. Many argue that if AI takes over artistic content, this might bring down the value of human creativity. And, as you know, human creativity and the emotion linked to a piece of art are unique and can't be emulated. This can also lead to another issue where AI is contributing to the homogenization of artistic styles and, with that, wearing away the different cultural expressions that make us different from one another and the different cultures we live in.

All of this can disrupt the creative industries and impact many people's lives, from writers to artists or musicians. It's crucial that we find a way to incorporate AI into the creative field, but more in a supporting role than taking over the field completely. However, there are some initiatives where human creativity and AI collaborate to improve efficiency and outcomes in the creative field. For example, AI can help artists and others in the artistic field become more productive and efficient when it comes to automating repetitive tasks, such as formatting.

It can also be an excellent partner when it comes to inspiration, where AI can assist creatives by giving them ideas or concepts. There are many other uses where AI can amplify human creativity; we just need to look at the unique characteristics of a person and couple them with the unique characteristics of AI to make work as well as the life of the creative a lot easier.

We've seen the potential AI can have in the most diverse industries in the near future, as well as the impact it's having now. We've talked about how AI is changing the finance and banking industries and what we can expect in the next few years as it continues to progress. From fraud detection to the analysis of behavior, there are many applications where AI can shine and make the field not only more profitable but also fairer for everyone. We've also seen the impact AI will have in the transport and logistics area, where autonomous vehicles are taking the lead, but also in the way it can change driving in cities through traffic management.

Vehicle congestion is a real problem in most of the world's big cities, and it's important that this gets addressed with the help of AI because it not only makes people's lives easier but also helps reduce emissions. AI is also completely changing the logistics sector, especially when it comes to the supply chain and how to make it more efficient. This has been a real problem as the world's population continues to grow and businesses have trouble figuring out ways to get goods to people. Not only can AI solve that, but it can also help businesses when it comes to inventory management, supplier management, or even risk assessment.

Lastly, we've talked about how AI is affecting the creative field, and while there are many great things happening, there are still numerous challenges that we need to overcome. Here, the key is to find the right balance where both human creatives and AI can collaborate without taking emotion and creativity from people. In the next chapter, we will dive into AI ethics and responsible AI, which is a subject that needs to be addressed as quickly as possible, so we can continue to progress in the AI field.

7

AI ETHICS AND RESPONSIBLE AI

Deepfake AI can manipulate audio, images, and videos so convincingly that people can't say if it's real or not. This is the reality we live in at the moment and can be quite scary. This is one of the reasons why we need to come up with responsible AI practices and ethics, so AI is not used to manipulate people in any form.

Ethics and responsible AI practices are also what we will be talking about in this chapter, where we will be discussing bias and fairness, governance and regulations, and what the future of responsible AI looks like.

BIAS AND FAIRNESS IN AI

We've briefly mentioned how bias and a lack of fairness can have an impact on society. This can lead to an amplification of inequality, unfair treatment, marginalization, or even the reinforcement of stereotypes. For example, looking at the amplification of inequality, this can easily be perceived in biased credit scoring from AI systems, where it might not give the same chance to people from disadvantaged backgrounds. This can also lead to unfair treatment when it comes to recruitment and hiring or even reinforce stereotypes, for example, in AI systems in criminal justice. But this leads to yet another problem, which is accountability in case these systems make mistakes.

To address some of these issues, there's a need for ethical frameworks that AI has to adhere to ensure fairness regardless of its tasks and diverse data to make sure AI is trained appropriately. In another chapter, I've highlighted transparency in the algorithm to understand how the AI came to such a decision. We need to understand that AI should be used for the good of the people, but if not used appropriately, it can have tremendous consequences in people's lives.

There are other methods that we can use to address these issues, in particular when it comes to bias and fairness, such as bias detection, where bias can be not only detected but also measured to understand the extent of the bias. The preprocessing system can also be optimized to make sure it encompasses a large range of different demographics, as well as reviewing all the processes. However, this has to be coupled with regular tests and audits to identify any unfairness or bias in the algorithms.

However, one of the best strategies we can use to tackle this issue is to have diverse and inclusive AI development teams, since these can play an important role when it comes to building these systems and ensuring that everything is fair. There are many benefits that can come from a diverse AI development team, such as avoiding homogeneous thinking. When a team is homogeneous, there's a lack of diversity in thinking, which often leads to points of view that are very similar, which in turn decreases creativity and the option for other solutions.

This would also help mitigate stereotypes by simply bringing people together who have had different life experiences and seeing the world with different eyes. This will not only present more diverse solutions to problems but also increase the market reach of AI systems and the underlying technology. If in a team there are people from different countries, for instance, all members can contribute with their different cultural norms, making the AI system easier to adopt by different cultures.

It's important to incorporate diversity, not only in AI development teams but in other teams in different sectors, not only from an ethical point of view but also because it helps solve problems or at least see challenges from a different point of view. AI systems are here to serve everyone equally and to make a positive contribution to society as a whole.

AI REGULATION AND GOVERNANCE

Of course, all of this has to be backed by proper regulation and governance to be able to be enforced. The need for regulation and governance in the AI field has become more apparent as AI continues to advance and is being incorporated into different sectors. Let's look at some of the most important reasons for regulation and governance.

Ethical concerns, data privacy, and fairness are all topics that we've already discussed but are particularly important when it comes to regulations. To get here, we might need to do things a little differently. For instance, public engagement might be of relevance here, especially when it comes to the policymaking processes to ensure these technologies are aligned with the needs and values of society. Regulations also need to help prevent the creation or deployment of AI systems that can cause harm to people, such as deepfakes.

When it comes to potential policy frameworks, there are numerous things that we need to look at. For instance, have industry standards and processes for certification to make sure that AI systems that are deployed meet certain criteria. It's also crucial that we establish guidelines when it comes to data collection and sharing to reduce issues with privacy.

However, because AI has many different applications in different sectors, we need to come up with regulations that make sense in those different sectors and not apply a "one-size-fits-all" type of regulation, which would certainly harm some of the industries and the people in them. Besides that, there's the need for international collaboration, so that every country can be part of the international standards for AI regulation.

We, as a society, need to find the right balance between encouraging innovation in the AI field and addressing the challenges by creating effective regulations that will allow us to do that.

There are a few challenges when it comes to the regulation of AI, especially because of how quickly the technology is evolving in some spaces. The main issue here is that the current regulatory approaches are insufficient and can't keep up with how fast technology spreads. In turn, for instance, this slows down the pace of innovation in the field. There are many breakthroughs in the AI space with the finding of more and more applications, but current regulatory processes take very long, which hinders that innovation.

Another issue is that AI is developing in many sectors and sub-sectors, such as ML, NLP, and even robotics, and because of this, there's no proper definition of what AI is and is not. There's an urgent need to set clear boundaries for what AI is and create regulations that encompass all of these subsets of AI. Regulators lack domain expertise, which means that they don't have a great technical understanding of the technology, which makes it increasingly difficult for them to create regulations and to create them effectively. There's a real need to close the gap and bring more experts into the regulatory processes, so things can flow faster and more accurately.

Of course, such fast development of technology has no precedent, which makes things a little more complex without a frame of reference. Because of that, regulators, coupled with their lack of expertise, have a hard time predicting risks as well as benefits from new applications in the AI field. We also have to take into account some unintended consequences of the fast deployment of AI systems and applications that will become more noticeable as they spread across the globe, which leads, once again, to a lack of predictability on their behalf and might set some applications of AI back.

All of this, coupled with the fairness, bias, and ethical concerns with which regulatory bodies continue to struggle, has a massive impact on regulating AI in different sectors. However, awareness and public engagement are essential, not only to keep the public informed but also to try and understand AI's implications, which is yet another challenge in such a fast-evolving field.

To address all of these issues, there's a need for an adaptable and flexible approach to regulations, as well as collaboration between AI developers, regulatory bodies, governments, and the people. Without this, the struggles we are going through right now in the AI space will continue to exist and will continue to hinder not only technology but also society.

This doesn't mean there haven't been some efforts at the international level to develop governance within the AI field, and these are gaining momentum. These efforts are doing all the right things, such as pleading for standard regulations, collaboration between governments, and ensuring that there are ethical and responsible AI practices, but, sometimes, these also fall short, although it is too early to say that they will fail. Let's look at some of these efforts.

The G20 AI principles are one of them. You might be familiar with the G20—the 20 most powerful countries, economically speaking—and they are trying to come up with a set of AI principles with the objective of addressing some of the issues we've been talking about here, such as transparency, promoting innovation, and so on. However, nothing concrete has come out of it yet, but it's one of the most promising initiatives in the AI space. Perhaps even more promising are the OECD principles on AI.

The OECD encompasses all the developed countries in the world, which is better than the G20 mainly because it encompasses more countries, and here they are trying to bring up the main principles that should be behind AI technology, such as accountability, transparency, respect for human rights, and so forth. The aim of these principles is to provide a foundation for all governments to start discussing AI governance.

There are others, such as the EU AI regulation, which focuses on essentially the same principles but is aimed at EU countries, or the UN AI Ethics Initiative, which focuses on ethics in the AI space. All of these are welcomed and highlight the international collaboration many countries are trying to achieve. While many are still in the drafting stage, they will certainly play an important role in the future when it comes to addressing some of the issues we've been having so far.

THE FUTURE OF RESPONSIBLE AI

There are many moving parts when it comes to the future of responsible AI that have to align for us to achieve that. One of those is organizations' and governments' role in promoting responsible AI. To do this, there's a need for establishing a proper regulatory framework with standards for how AI development should progress and be used, while at the same time adhering to any ethical principles. Here, defined ethical guidelines will also make an impact as well as promote accountability, transparency, and fairness.

However, there's also a need for investment in development and research if governments are to be responsible for AI use and deployment. This investment has to come directly from the government and focus on the challenges at hand. By supporting such projects, they will also be spreading responsible AI within the population. But, governments have to go a little beyond that and be able to collaborate and make private partnerships with industries and academia, so AI can develop responsibly.

This allows for the sharing of knowledge and coming up with fair policies. Besides that, there's a need for a campaign where governments and other organizations need to raise awareness about responsible practices and ethics in AI, and this can be done in the form of workshops, seminars, or education campaigns.

Only by working together can both governments and private organizations make sure AI is developed responsibly and aligns with the values of society. This is a collaborative effort that requires commitment from all parties involved.

Let's now see what ethical considerations are needed when it comes to AI research and development. I'm not going to explore some of the ethical considerations I've already talked about in the book, such as fairness and bias, transparency, accountability, or privacy, but there are others that need attention too. For instance, one that we haven't talked about is social impact. It's important that we focus on the broader impact of AI applications, so we don't increase the already existing inequalities that we have, which would cause even more harm.

In the same way that AI can have the impact of broadening inequalities, it also has the power to minimize them. For this, the development of AI and especially training have to be done properly, such as training on unbiased data and collecting diverse data. If we are not careful and ignore the impacts of AI, we can have job displacement or economic disruptions because AI could create a massive economic shift that our society would not be able to handle. Governments, as well as AI developers, need to understand the negative impacts of AI and make efforts to mitigate them.

Another ethical consideration governments and developers have to take into account is the dual-use concern. This simply means that while AI has the potential to do good, some AI systems might be purposefully used to do harm. There has to be a deep assessment of how to avoid

AI systems being used to cause harm and malicious activities, such as misinformation, for instance.

Another thing to consider is the long-term effects of AI technologies not only on society or the economy but also on workers. AI systems and development should contribute positively to social well-being and economic growth, but we need to do our research and try to find out what our world will look like in 10, 15, or 20 years if AI continues to advance. We need to be prepared for what is coming and establish regulations to avoid any long-term negative impacts AI might have on our society.

Continued monitoring and improvement will be necessary because it's hard to fully understand the full impact of new AI applications in our society. We need to make adjustments as we go to make sure we are not caught off guard and spiral into negative consequences that might be irreversible.

We've discussed how important ethical AI is and how relevant its role is and will continue to be in the future of technology. But, as we've also seen, AI technology can also be used for malice, such as manipulation of images, videos, and audio, or deepfakes. That's why I emphasize responsible practices and ethical AI, so we can avoid harmful situations coming not only from AI developers but also from governments in the form of guidelines on how to deploy AI applications. There's a need for diverse AI development teams, so we can mitigate the risks of AI systems becoming biased or unfair toward certain people.

But, of course, there are many challenges that we need to overcome when it comes to regulating AI, which is rapidly evolving and being incorporated into society without these regulations and guidelines. Not only do we have to come up with these, but we also need to predict what other impacts they might have on our society in the future, as well as make constant monitoring and adjustments to those practices and regulations. We need an international effort in AI governance, and although we've taken some exciting initiatives, we still have a long way to go to make these come true. The problem is that we need them now and not in a couple of years because of how quickly AI is developing. We need to apply ethical and responsible practices as fast as we can to ensure AI has a positive impact on our society, while at the same time minimizing any potential harm. If we want to continue the positive things that AI brings us, we need to come up with a way to ensure no one is penalized by the technology.

8

AI AND SOCIETY—OPPORTUNITIES AND CHALLENGES

According to a study, the IT and telecommunication sector has the highest adoption rate in the AI sector with 29.5%, which is followed by the legal sector with 29.2% (Hooson, 2023). This is a sign that AI has many applications in many different sectors. However, I will start with the challenges before moving on to the opportunities it brings to society.

THE IMPACT OF AI ON JOBS

When it comes to the negative impact of AI on jobs, automation is perhaps the biggest challenge, which often leads to job displacement. This has been widely debated over the years since the incorporation of AI in different sectors, but here are some of the things we, as a society, need to consider, especially when it comes to job displacement.

For instance, many jobs involve routines that are repetitive, and those are the ones that are more likely to be replaced with automation. In this case, administrative jobs, line work, or even data processing are the types of jobs that are more susceptible to this change and to being displaced.

While at the start, AI focused on blue-collar jobs, it is now coming after white-collar jobs such as data analysts or any other job that involves routine and cognitive tasks. As some of these jobs are automated by AI, there's a need for workers to either reskill or upskill, but these initiatives and programs have to come from the companies themselves in order to help workers adapt to new functions.

Now, some ways to stop this have to do with an increase in human-AI collaboration, and many vouch for this to happen. In the same way that AI assists workers, they should be able to assist AI too, whether it is monitoring or making sure the data input is accurate, as well as looking out for any issues such as bias or a lack of transparency in AI systems. It's probable that the job landscape will be much more dynamic than it was until now, and so the emphasis will be on workers becoming more skilled as well as more adaptable to new roles.

However, it's also relevant to note that the impact of AI on jobs is different in every sector, and while some sectors might experience more disruption, others might not feel it as much. The important thing here is to be able to find a balance, so we minimize job displacement and reduce unemployment throughout all industries.

AI Augmentation in the Workforce

AI augmentation is a concept whereby, by using AI systems and devices, we can expand human capabilities and, instead of replacing workers and humans, we are amplifying their abilities. This is one of the most promising concepts when it comes to collaboration between humans and AI systems. Within this concept, AI is a tool that is leveraged to empower people in their work, which in turn makes them more efficient in their tasks. This concept tries to bring the best of both worlds when it comes to AI systems and humans. You might be wondering exactly how AI augmentation works. Well, let's see some of the main aspects of it.

AI augmentation allows for improved decision-making. This means that, as you know, AI can quickly analyze a large volume of data and, with that, inform the worker of the best possible decision. It can also automate repetitive tasks and allow more time for the worker to pursue other, more creative tasks. It also allows the enhancement of the worker's cognitive abilities through the quick analysis of data from the AI system, allowing the worker to understand insights better and take important information from it quickly.

Another important aspect of this is how AIs can act as experts in a field and advise the worker. This often happens in the healthcare and medical fields, but also in the legal sector or even in scientific research. There's a lot of promise in AI augmentation because it not only empowers workers but also allows them to collaborate with AI systems that improve their outcomes and don't displace or even replace them.

But now I want to discuss something that has to happen as augmented AI is incorporated into places of work: upskilling and reskilling. These will be viral methods to prepare workers and adapt to the many changes that will happen. There's no way around it; AI is here to stay, and we have to be able to adapt to it quickly and efficiently, which means that we will need to retrain some of our skills. It's not only adapting that will be important but also addressing skill gaps that we might have once AI is introduced into the workplace.

It's possible that AI coming into the workplace will create some gaps inside businesses because current jobs will have to either evolve or simply disappear, which will prompt workers to either reskill or upskill. While reskilling means learning a completely new skill and perhaps doing a completely different role from what workers are doing now, upskilling means improving existing skills to be able to adapt to the new change.

It's also important to work on soft skills, and this is usually something that AI cannot do because it involves human interaction, such as in creative roles or customer service. This should be part of the upskilling training since AI will probably take over those tasks where soft skills are not used.

While reskilling might seem a little scarier because we would have to learn a completely new skill, it can also be seen as an opportunity to change careers and get into industries that we never thought we would be working in. This gains special emphasis if you reskill into an emerging field that is linked to AI, such as ML or data science, where there's a margin to progress.

When it comes to upskilling, an interesting aspect of it is that because it involves something more "human," such as the improvement of soft skills, the tendency is to have an increase in employment engagement. Humans are social, and improving these skills will make their social lives better, and with that, more engagement on their behalf.

While companies should be in charge of reskilling and upskilling programs, they don't have to do this alone. In fact, they should seek collaboration with educational institutions and develop partnerships where employees can upskill or reskill, while at the same time, these educational institutions make sure what the employees learn aligns with the standards of the industry and what the industry is looking for. So, upskilling and reskilling will be essential to working collaboratively with AI systems and improving the outcomes of businesses. But, this investment will also ensure that the impact on job displacement will be minimized.

AI AND SOCIAL IMPLICATIONS

We will go back to one of the problems we talked about at the start of the book that has to do with the impact AI might have on privacy and data security, how it can influence social dynamics and human interaction, and the potential AI has to address societal challenges such as climate change.

We've already talked about data privacy, tracking, surveillance, data breaches, bias, and discrimination, which are all social implications that we should be concerned about as AI gets integrated into our society. However, in this section, I'm going to talk about strategies to address some of these problems. One of these strategies should be the collection and retention of only the necessary data that is essential for AI training, which allows for people's personal data to be less exposed.

Education on this topic is also something that we should invest in, particularly in educating people about the risks as well as the benefits of AI and their rights to maintain sensible data protection. But this has to be done with some of the other strategies we've already talked about, such as a proper regulatory framework, ethical oversight, transparency, and privacy.

We also have to highlight AI's influence on social dynamics and human interaction. The more AI systems' use increases across many industries, the more its impact on our lives, and so we can expect this impact to be felt in human interaction and social dynamics. However, this is not always a bad thing and has many positives as well. For example, remote work and collaboration between people working in different places.

There are many AI tools that allow for this collaboration between remote workers to be as smooth as possible and just as effective or even more effective than working side-by-side in an office. Some of these tools involve project management or real-time communication, for instance. Other impacts might be neutral, depending on the person, of course. For instance, one of the things we've talked about is algorithmic recommendation, whether this is on social media to show posts that we might be more interested in or on platforms such as Netflix or Spotify.

While some people welcome these, others might frown upon them, but either way, this reaches a level of personalization that we've never seen before. The same goes for online shopping, and here we also have mixed opinions on it. While some people like the fact that an algorithm understands what they would like to buy, others believe it is just a plot for organizations to sell more.

But then, there are the negative impacts, such as deepfakes or misinformation, which I think everyone can agree has a negative impact on our society. This is because it is becoming more and more challenging to authenticate if an image or a video is true or fake, which might have massive repercussions for people. Misinformation is another negative impact, where fabricated news or content, in general, can wear out the trust the public has in people or organizations and even sway whole opinions.

As AI evolves, its impact will continue to progress, and we will notice it more and more. While, as we've seen, there are many benefits and advantages to it, there are also negative impacts. Once again, we need to mitigate those negative impacts and create a balance between the two.

How Can We Use AI to Address Societal Challenges?

While AI can have a relevant role in addressing some of society's challenges, I'll be talking about one issue in particular that has been plaguing society for quite a while and for which we don't seem to have a clear solution as of now: climate change.

If we look at AI's strengths, such as pattern recognition and data analysis, we can understand what a powerful tool AI is and its potential when it comes to mitigating the outcomes of climate change. For instance, when it comes to the solutions we have found to reduce the impact of climate change, renewable energy seems to be a good option; however, we have been failing to integrate it properly into our society. AI can help with that by allowing a better reintegration of these systems, such as wind power or solar power, into the energy grid.

This is because AI can analyze and predict energy generation and, with that, ensure a sustainable energy supply. It can also help us manage this energy in a more efficient way by optimizing energy consumption in the many industries of our society, such as manufacturing or transportation. But one of the best ways AI can help us is to create climate models that will allow scientists and researchers to understand the complexity of climate systems, predict outcomes, and identify the real impacts of climate change.

Agricultural and food security through agricultural practices and their optimization is another way where AI can shine, which can lead to more sustainable farming methods. Smart grids are also something that exists but is yet to be fully adopted by those who have them. With AI's help, we can optimize energy distribution and respond to current demand by analyzing data and allowing AI to make adjustments to supply and demand.

However, most of these are mere ideas talked about and have yet to be put into practice. And even though these are not long-term solutions, there's a need for a global effort to reduce emissions and find long-term solutions.

AI AND GLOBAL COLLABORATION

It's no secret that we need global collaboration when it comes to developing and deploying AI systems in the most diverse industries while causing the least negative impact on our society. But, yes, to achieve that, we need countries and governments across the world to work together to solve many of the issues that we are facing. Let's look at the main reasons why global collaboration is essential when it comes to integrating AI.

Well, for one, global collaboration will accelerate progress in the field. It's known that the sharing of knowledge between developers and researchers leads to faster and better results. If we collaborate globally, we can reach a solution for problems such as fairness or bias in AI a lot faster, and we don't have to do double or triple the work to get there. Plus, we would have a standardized regulation and ethics plan that would suit everyone.

Global collaboration would also ensure that there would be access to resources since such projects need a significant amount of infrastructure or computational resources. If we put all our efforts together, we can share those resources and cut the cost of projects. We would also have perspectives from everybody in the world, which would ensure we would have no biases within the AI systems. This would also allow the exchange of talent, which would speed up some projects.

While global collaboration can come in many different forms, it's important for us to take the first steps in doing this. We would tackle many of the issues we have now simply by working together. Of course, this is far easier said than done, but we are getting to the point where we will have to make a decision, and everything indicates that international collaboration is the right path to follow.

Now, we will turn to another global challenge, which is the healthcare crisis, and how AI's role can have an impact on it. As you know, AI has a lot of potential when it comes to finding solutions in the healthcare sector, but we need, once again, a global effort.

There are many challenges in the healthcare sector, such as faster diagnosis, better patient care, and faster ways to trial and discover drugs. But besides those, AI can do so much more. For instance, with the technology we have today, we can monitor patients remotely. We have wearables that can track patients' vitals and many other important metrics, and most of these are equipped with AI systems that can analyze data quickly and alert for anything that might be wrong.

I'm sure everyone knows about the COVID-19 pandemic that not only froze the entire world but also killed many people. AI can help not only with the management of these outbreaks but also predict them. This informs not only the public but also the authorities on how to act and manage these outbreaks. Virtual health assistants, which can simply be chatbots that give patients personalized advice and can answer many questions they might have, or even telemedicine, which is something that has been on the rise, allow patients to attend remote consultations, which allows those in areas far from hospitals and clinics to have the medical attention they need.

The role of AI in the healthcare crisis is perhaps one of the most important ones and promises to completely shift the sector for the better and overcome many of the challenges we have today.

There are some success stories that highlight AI's global collaboration. For instance, during the COVID-19 pandemic, there was a global collaboration among AI researchers as well as medical professionals to quickly understand what type of virus we were dealing with as well as how it spread. AI systems analyzed data and predicted infection rates, which accelerated the development of a vaccine.

Another success story in AI global collaboration was the European Organization for Nuclear Research (CERN), which, when built, was a great collaboration between many scientists across the world. Nowadays, AI is used to analyze the generated data related to the understanding of how these particles behave.

As you can tell, there are many opportunities for AI when it comes to social impact, but there are also many different challenges that we need to overcome. AI has the power to change all of that. We've seen its impact on the job market, where the introduction of AI raised many concerns, especially when it came to job displacement. But we now have some solutions to it that involve collaboration between AI systems and workers, as well as the reskilling and upskilling of other workers.

There needs to be collaboration between the two if we don't want to create a negative impact in that sector of our society. AI augmentation is another point in favor of collaboration between AI and employees, where the latter can exponentially improve their abilities and become much more effective. There's an urgent need to empower employees through AI tools, and this is the right path to follow instead of trying to replace them.

However, the concerns don't end here. The integration of AI in many different sectors also raises ethical and social concerns, such as lack of privacy, lack of transparency, bias, misinformation, and others that we've discussed in the chapter. I've also pointed out some of the strategies that we need to start integrating to overcome these issues and reach a balance that positively impacts society.

We've also seen how AI can address some other issues that we've not been able to solve in the past, such as climate change. The strength of AI is in analysis and finding patterns, and this is exactly what it should be used for by analyzing real-time data and indicating possible solutions.

For all of this, there's a need for global collaboration when it comes to AI deployment and research, so we can not only accelerate the process but also reach a balance where everyone is positively impacted by this advancement. The transformative potential of AI has its challenges, but we need to focus on how to overcome these and highlight the positives that will come out of it, which are tremendous. It's all about balancing ethics and well-being with the progress we would make as a society.

9

AI AND THE HUMAN-MACHINE INTERFACE

One of the main questions that is on everyone's mind is: How can human-AI collaboration reevaluate the limits of creativity and problem-solving in ways that we or AI could do alone? That's the question many AI researchers have been pondering for the last few years, and the answer is human-machine interface.

EXPLAINABLE AI

Explainable AI (XAI), is a relatively new concept where AI is developed to clearly explain to us how it got there. So far, we have been having an issue with it, which is called the "black box problem," where AI reaches outcomes but cannot fully explain to us how it got there.

We've already discussed the importance of transparency when it comes to AI decision-making, so we will focus on

XAI; in particular, the challenges and opportunities in building XAI models.

Starting with challenges, the complexity of the models is one of them. Some of the most complex AI models we have today, such as DL models, are extremely complex and have many different layers, which makes it extremely challenging for AI to provide clear explanations for some of their decisions.

Some researchers believe that if we set up AI systems to explain how they reach certain results, this will be a trade-off when it comes to overall performance because, for us to understand their decisions, we would have to make these systems less complex, which would have a negative impact on the outcome. Another challenge might be the consistency of those explanations, where different outcomes might be a little more difficult to explain.

However, there are also many opportunities to build an XAI. For instance, if we know exactly how AI systems reached certain outcomes, this means that they would be within regulatory compliance. This is because most industries require full transparency as well as accountability for whatever decisions the AI systems make. There would also be more acceptance and trust in AI systems because of the clear explanation they would give us, which is extremely important when it comes to sectors such as finance or healthcare. In the educational field, this would also be a great opportunity because we could use the explanations to help others understand how processes work.

There are already many real-world examples of XAI in practice. For example, in the context of autonomous vehicles, many decisions made by AI are explainable, such as why they've applied the brakes or why they might have changed lanes. But also in the financial sector, we've seen XAI in practice, in particular, how AI deals with loan approval decisions.

In this case, it's very important that an explanation be provided, especially if the loan approval is denied. The same is true for content recommendations, where platforms such as YouTube or Netflix use these systems. In fact, on many of these platforms, they explain to you the commonality found between the shows or videos you've watched and what the algorithm is recommending to you.

These are just some examples of how XAI techniques are being applied in the real world across different sectors.

AI AND HUMAN CREATIVITY

As you know, AI systems and algorithms have been used in design, music, and even art with many different applications. But they've also been used frequently in the movie industry, helping with visual effects and animation.

In the marketing and advertising field to target an accurate section of the market through the analysis of data, or even in video game development. But when it comes to creativity, AI can help human creativity in many different ways. For example, in cooking, where an AI-powered recipe generator could potentially aid chefs in coming up with new dishes, or in scientific research by quickly analyzing large volumes of data.

While AI can help come up with ideas, the human part of it, such as emotional depth and understanding of cultural context, is unique to humans and something AI cannot mimic. With this, what I mean to say is that humans and AI systems can work collaboratively to reach better creative outcomes.

AI is already spreading fast through some of these creative fields, and the reception wasn't always positive. There's always an initial skepticism from the creatives themselves, but also curiosity from the public and even from these creatives about how AI can help them reach new heights. The initial skepticism also came from the fact that they feared how accurately AI could emulate human emotion, which it turns out that it can't, but now there's the issue of copyrights and infringing intellectual property that needs to be dealt with.

However, not everything is bad, and AI systems, as they continue to make progress, have allowed creatives to start to experiment with the technology and the ability to create new forms of art. Because the art industry was where AI entered first, we can now see much more collaboration than in other industries, which led to the amplification of human creativity.

Of course, there are also many challenges that need to be overcome, especially when it comes to originality and authenticity, and it's important to debate this and set clear boundaries. So, besides the initial skepticism, this progressed to experimentation and even curiosity, and it will still take some time to become fully accepted, but it's on the right path.

AI AND EMOTIONAL INTELLIGENCE

Now, you might not make the connection between AI and emotional intelligence; after all, I've emphasized the lack of emotion or cultural context in AI systems. AI has the potential to understand human emotions as well as social cues, which is, in fact, one of the biggest advancements in the AI field. This has tremendous implications in the most diverse fields, from human-machine interaction to customer service or even mental health.

AI has the ability to recognize tone of voice, facial expressions, and even emotion in text content. This is done through auditory and visual cues, and after being analyzed, it can accurately understand certain emotions. But how does this apply to the different fields? Well, let's start with mental health. In this field, AI can make emotional analyses of mental health care and allow mental health professionals to understand certain patterns, such as anxiety. In human-machine interaction, AI, by understanding these emotions, can seamlessly find the balance between human and machine.

We've already talked about how social media can be a big source of analysis for the sentiments of customers through their interactions on social media platforms. This is extremely important for market research and advertising, as well as for businesses to understand what customers want. While we are still a little far from realizing all the capabilities of emotional intelligence in AI, this is a continuous improvement that will become better as more data is fed into AI systems and more adjustments are made by developers. But, in conclusion, the potential AI has for understanding human emotion and other social cues is extremely important because it has the ability to change people's lives.

The ethical challenges here come from the fact that there might be bias and inaccuracy in the results of some assessments. Another issue that is often raised is a lack of contextual understanding when interpreting these emotions. Most of the time, people can only understand others' emotions when given context. However, this is something that AI systems might have trouble with because they might lack an understanding of this human context, which might lead to inaccuracies in assessments.

There are ethical considerations that we also have to highlight, such as emotional manipulation, for instance. This means that because AI might be able to understand emotions, it can also be used with the malicious intent of manipulating those emotions. Another ethical challenge comes from AI in the mental health space, where it needs to be fed sensitive information in order to make accurate assessments, but this needs to be handled responsibly or, once again, might be used for malicious purposes.

The long-term effects of AI being able to analyze human emotions might also have an impact, and it's something often discussed. We need to make sure that if there are long-term impacts, these are positive and aligned with ethical principles.

The future of human-AI relationships is where we should be focusing as AI evolves, and, as we've seen, there are many applications for it. Collaboration between the two instead of the replacement of humans in the workplace is fundamental, especially once augmented human capabilities continue to be developed. We can not only find common ground to work side-by-side with AI but also improve the outcomes of the tasks we perform. This is also valid for creative collaboration, where we are far more advanced when it comes to this symbiosis between human and machine.

In the future, jobs will evolve, and we will have to either upskill or reskill to keep up, but it's important that we make these changes and embrace this new emerging technology. It's also plausible that different cultures will integrate AI in different ways, which will lead to different approaches, but with global collaboration, we can enjoy these new approaches and incorporate them into our own.

Once again, finding the right balance between embracing AI's potential and safeguarding our ethics and values is very important and the only way forward. The future of human-AI interaction is definitely an interesting topic and has many different implications for us as a society. From culture to economy and even ethics, AI technology is still quite young, and the more we interact with it, the more it will start shaping our lives.

In the financial and economic fields, job displacement due to automation is a serious concern, and we need to invest in reskilling and upskilling our workforce, so we can cope with the changes. However, this will also bring new job opportunities for many, especially in emerging fields such as ML and AI, which will ultimately contribute to the growth of the overall economy. Within the workforce itself, collaboration between workers and AI will be allowed through AI augmentation, which will improve productivity.

In the social and cultural impact of the future of human-AI interaction, we've seen so far a division between those who embrace and explore new ways of doing things, such as in some fields within the arts, but there's still some skepticism, and this is bound to happen as AI enters other industries. Data privacy is still an issue, and it's raising many concerns; however, once we reach a standard of regulation and ethics, we will be able to overcome this. The same is true for fairness and bias within AI algorithms; we, as a society, need to ensure that these are as far as possible through the many methods I've highlighted in this and past chapters.

CONCLUSION

> *"Instead of worrying about what AI can't do, it's more productive to think about what it can do to make our lives better"*
> –Max Tegmark

Now that we have the end of the book, it's important to highlight the message that we need to embrace curiosity and continuous learning in AI for many of the reasons I've pointed out throughout this journey. As AI evolves, there will be new applications as well as solutions that we need to be ready to embrace in the most varied industries.

Embracing this curiosity will set us up for incredible new things. It will bring new opportunities and personal and professional growth. It will make us more adaptable and more creative. If we do things right, AI will become one of the most impactful technologies we've experienced, with the potential to turn our world and our society for the better.

It's extremely important that we stay up-to-date with AI advancements because it will allow us to continue to evolve and to continue to better our lives. For us, as an individual, it's important to stay updated with AI advances because it means that we will continue to be relevant in the job market and will be able to continue to improve both professionally and personally. Besides that, if we keep up with AI advancement, we are pretty much safeguarding our future because AI's influence will only increase over time.

AI can be so impactful that it can solve real-world problems, and we should embrace it in that regard. It not only unleashes our creativity but will empower our efficiency. It will completely innovate industries and create new ones. It can help us solve challenging issues such as inequality, racism, climate change, and many others.

We can harness the power of AI to promote empathy between different cultures, promote inclusivity, break down barriers, and bridge the gaps that separate us. The world is changing, and leveraging AI to solve real-world problems is the best path to follow. By embracing AI, you can be part of the change to make this a better world.

In this book, we've seen how far AI has come from its origins in the 1950s with Alan Turing's test and the many setbacks and milestones it has achieved to be where it is today, and from the emergence of ML to the lack of computational power and the development of different

CONCLUSION

types of AI, such as narrow AI and general AI. We've also seen the many applications that emerged from AI and the many different industries that began to be incorporated into it with fantastic results.

We explored the ins and outs of ML and the different methods there are when it comes to training AI, such as supervised, unsupervised, and reinforcement learning. We've looked at the symbiotic relationship between data and AI and how important it is that we've become technologically capable of attaining large volumes of data. Also, we focused on how we've constructed neural networks that work similarly to how the human brain does.

In the last few years, we've experimented with AI in our daily lives, and many of us use AI without even knowing it. It's in our homes, our phones, and our cars, and sometimes, we even have conversations with AIs without even realizing it. It has been a seamless introduction to our lives. But we would have never gotten here without overcoming some challenges. To continue to advance, we will have to overcome others that are plaguing the AI industry now, such as responsible practices and ethical values.

It's important to strike a balance between these and still allow AI to be developed and continue to help us as we progress as a species. We've seen its impact on our finance and banking industries, in our transportation and logistics industries, and even in how it adapts to the creative fields. There are some issues that we need to address, and some are quite urgent, such as AI regulation and governance, bias and fairness, and what the future of responsible AI looks like, but this can only be attained through global collaboration, through a standardized regulation that will ensure that our values and ethics are not compromised.

But besides all of that, AI should mean new opportunities not only for us as individuals but for increased collaboration between different countries and governments. It's time to set our differences aside and collaborate with the help of AI because there are some issues that we can only overcome when we try to achieve good things for all of us. AI has to be seen as a tool for innovation and positive change, not as something that will take our jobs or invade our privacy.

Navigate the journey of exploring the innovation of limitless technology and endless opportunities. Make sure curiosity is with you, and allow AI to change our world for the better. But you also have the power to make changes through AI by embracing it and being ready for a future with AI. Constant growth is the most important thing in a world where AI is inevitable.

BIBLIOGRAPHY

AIContentfy Team. (2023, June 27). *AI vs human creativity: Which one will win?* AIContentfy. https://aicontentfy.com/en/blog/ai-vs-human-creativity-which-one-will-win

Al-Masri, A. (2022, October 31). *Backpropagation in a neural network: Explained.* Built In. https://builtin.com/machine-learning/backpropagation-neural-network

Altexsoft. (2021, April 14). *Unsupervised learning: Algorithms and examples.* https://www.altexsoft.com/blog/unsupervised-machine-learning

Amazon Web Services. (n.d.). *What is data labeling?* https://aws.amazon.com/sagemaker/data-labeling/what-is-data-labeling

Analytics Vidhya. (2019, April 18). *Introduction to deep Q-learning for reinforcement learning (in Python).* https://www.analyticsvidhya.com/blog/2019/04/introduction-deep-q-learning-python

Anyoha, R. (2017, August 28). *The history of artificial intelligence.* Science in the News, Harvard University. https://sitn.hms.harvard.edu/flash/2017/history-artificial-intelligence

AyaData. (2023, August 3). *Data acquisition for machine learning explained.* https://www.ayadata.ai/blog-posts/comprehensive-guide-to-data-acquisition-for-machine-learning

Azevedo, N. (n.d.). *6 techniques of data preprocessing.* Scalable Path. https://www.scalablepath.com/data-science/data-preprocessing-phase

Baxter, K. (2021, August 24). *What is AI bias mitigation, and how can it improve AI fairness?* InfoWorld. https://www.infoworld.com/article/3630450/what-is-ai-bias-mitigation-and-how-can-it-improve-ai-fairness.html

Bron, D. (2023, March 28). *Emotional AI: How machines are learning to understand and respond to human emotions.* LinkedIn. https://www.linkedin.com/pulse/emotional-ai-how-machines-learning-understand-respond-bron

Caruana, V. (2023, July 18). *The importance of explainability in AI decision-making.* Algolia. https://www.algolia.com/blog/ai/what-is-

BIBLIOGRAPHY

explainable-ai-and-why-is-transparency-so-important-for-machine-learning-solutions

Coursera. (2022, September 14). *3 types of machine learning you should know.* https://www.coursera.org/articles/types-of-machine-learning

Coursera. (2023, June 15). *AI ethics: What it is and why it matters.* https://www.coursera.org/articles/ai-ethics

Crosling, M. (2023, January 19). *Why are AI-enabled smart home products the next big thing?* Xailient. https://xailient.com/blog/why-are-ai-enabled-smart-home-products-the-next-big-thing

Data Dynamics. (2023, June 28). *7 reasons why AI is transforming the energy sector.* https://www.datadynamicsinc.com/blog-ai-in-energy-your-data-is-the-game-changer-7-reasons-why

DatabaseTown. (2023, May 27). *Unsupervised learning: Types, applications & advantages.* https://databasetown.com/unsupervised-learning-types-applications

DeAngelis, S. F. (2014, September 5). *Artificial intelligence: How algorithms make systems smart.* Wired. https://www.wired.com/insights/2014/09/artificial-intelligence-algorithms-2

Drugeot, C. (n.d.). *The importance of big data and cloud computing.* DevOps Online. https://www.devopsonline.co.uk/the-importance-of-big-data-and-cloud-computing

FLR Spectron. (2021, January 27). *More data has been created in the past two years than in the entire history of humanity.* https://www.flrs.co.uk/more-data-has-been-created-in-the-past-two-years-than-in-the-entire-history-of-humanity

Gavrilova, Y. (2021, December 10). *Anomaly detection in machine learning.* Serokell. https://serokell.io/blog/anomaly-detection-in-machine-learning

Goasduff, L. (2019, July 31). *Chatbots will appeal to modern workers.* Gartner. https://www.gartner.com/smarterwithgartner/chatbots-will-appeal-to-modern-workers

Gow, G. (2022, October 30). *The argument for an AI augmented workforce.* Forbes. https://www.forbes.com/sites/glenngow/2022/10/30/the-argument-for-an-ai-augmented-workforce/?sh=1fe0cce72f4c

Great Learning Team. (2020, April 29). *Types of neural networks and definition of neural network.* Great Learning. https://www.mygreatlearning.com/blog/types-of-neural-networks

Greene, G. (n.d.). *The ethics of AI and emotional intelligence data sources, applications, and questions for evaluating ethics risk*. https://partnershiponai.org/wp-content/uploads/2021/08/PAI_The-ethics-of-AI-and-emotional-intelligence_073020.pdf

Hardesty, L. (2017, April 14). *Explained: Neural networks*. MIT News. https://news.mit.edu/2017/explained-neural-networks-deep-learning-0414

Hooson, M. (2023, August 11). *UK artificial intelligence (AI) statistics and trends in 2023*. Forbes Advisor UK. https://www.forbes.com/uk/advisor/business/software/uk-artificial-intelligence-ai-statistics-2023

IBM. (n.d.). *What is a data set?* https://www.ibm.com/docs/en/zos-basic-skills?topic=more-what-is-data-set

IBM. (2021). *What are neural networks?* https://www.ibm.com/topics/neural-networks

IBM. (2023a). *What is machine learning?* https://www.ibm.com/topics/machine-learning

IBM. (2023b). *What is supervised learning?* https://www.ibm.com/topics/supervised-learning

Jagalapoordi, S. (2023, April 7). *Exploring the importance and techniques of hyperparameter tuning in machine learning*. LinkedIn. https://www.linkedin.com/pulse/exploring-importance-techniques-hyperparameter-tuning-jagarlapoodi

Johnson, J. (2020, September 16). *Anomaly detection with machine learning: An introduction*. BMC Blogs. https://www.bmc.com/blogs/machine-learning-anomaly-detection

Khan, R. (2022, October 12). *Impact of artificial intelligence on our everyday life*. ProjectCubicle. https://www.projectcubicle.com/impact-of-artificial-intelligence-on-our-everyday-life

Kiran, B. R., Sobh, I., Talpaert, V., Mannion, P., Sallab, A. A. A., Yogamani, S., & Perez, P. (2021). Deep reinforcement learning for autonomous driving: A survey. *IEEE Transactions on Intelligent Transportation Systems, 23*(6), 4909–4926. https://doi.org/10.1109/tits.2021.3054625

KnowledgeHut. (n.d.). *Big data technologies that everyone should know in 2023*. https://www.knowledgehut.com/blog/big-data/big-data-technologies

Kumar, A. (2022, August 19). *Recommender systems in machine learning:*

BIBLIOGRAPHY

Examples. Data Analytics. https://vitalflux.com/recommender-systems-in-machine-learning-examples

Madill, W. (2022, April 20). *Exploring natural language processing (NLP)*. Localize. https://localizejs.com/articles/natural-language-processing-nlp

Mahendru, R. (2023, April 27). *"AI won't take your job but humans who learn AI will"- Kai-Fu Lee*. LinkedIn. https://www.linkedin.com/pulse/ai-wont-take-your-job-humans-who-learn-will-kai-fu-lee-mahendru

Mbaabu, O. (2020, November 18). *Clustering in unsupervised machine learning*. Section. https://www.section.io/engineering-education/clustering-in-unsupervised-ml

Miller, R. (2019, December 13). *Data preprocessing: What is it and why is important?* CEOWORLD Magazine. https://ceoworld.biz/2019/12/13/data-preprocessing-what-is-it-and-why-is-important

NetApp. (n.d.). *AI for computer vision applications*. https://www.netapp.com/artificial-intelligence/computer-vision

Robotnik. (2022, April 29). *Use and applications of artificial intelligence in robotics*. https://robotnik.eu/introduction-to-robotics-and-artificial-intelligence

Rouse, M. (2023, July 5). *What is data set?* Techopedia. https://www.techopedia.com/definition/3348/data-set-ibm-mainframe

Sajid, H. (n.d.). *AI in robotics: 6 groundbreaking applications*. V7labs. https://www.v7labs.com/blog/ai-in-robotics

The Science of Machine Learning. (n.d.). *Exponential growth*. https://www.ml-science.com/exponential-growth

Simplilearn. (2021, March 29). *Challenges of big data: Basic concepts, case study, and more*. https://www.simplilearn.com/challenges-of-big-data-article

Statt, N. (2019, April 13). *OpenAI's Dota 2 AI steamrolls world champion e-sports team with back-to-back victories*. The Verge. https://www.theverge.com/2019/4/13/18309459/openai-five-dota-2-finals-ai-bot-competition-og-e-sports-the-international-champion

Tableau. (n.d.). *8 natural language processing (NLP) examples*. https://www.tableau.com/learn/articles/natural-language-processing-examples

Thormundsson, B. (2022). *Global AI software market size 2018–2025*.

Statista. https://www.statista.com/statistics/607716/worldwide-artificial-intelligence-market-revenues

Toney, A. (2021, August 11). *Defining computer vision, natural language processing, and robotics research clusters.* Center for Security and Emerging Technology. https://cset.georgetown.edu/publication/defining-computer-vision-natural-language-processing-and-robotics-research-clusters

University of York. (2021, December 20). *What is reinforcement learning?* https://online.york.ac.uk/what-is-reinforcement-learning

University of York. (2022, May 23). *How do algorithms work?* https://online.york.ac.uk/how-do-algorithms-work

Valcheva, S. (2018, March 11). *Supervised vs unsupervised learning: Algorithms, example, difference.* Intellspot. https://www.intellspot.com/unsupervised-vs-supervised-learning

Wisdom, D. (2023, June 30). *What is natural language processing and how does it work?* Datalink Networks. https://www.datalinknetworks.net/dln_blog/what-is-natural-language-processing-and-how-does-it-work

Yadav, A. (2022, September 22). *The role played by cloud computing in big data.* Datafloq. https://datafloq.com/read/the-role-played-by-cloud-computing-in-big-data

Printed in Great Britain
by Amazon